Secrets:

Florida Writers Association Collection, Volume 15

Secrets:

Florida Writers Association Collection, Volume 15

Published by:
Florida Writers Association
127 W. Fairbanks Ave. #407
Winter Park FL 32789

First edition: October 2023

Print ISBN: 978-1-7375305-3-4
eBook ISBN: 978-1-7375305-4-1
Library of Congress Control Number: 2023940312

Cover Design: Ginnye Cubel
Copy Editing: Paul Iasevoli and Arielle Haughee
Interior Formatting: Autumn Skye

Printed in the United States of America

Table of Contents

NextGen Writers

Secrets Revealed:

A Note from the Chair

When I was initially approached to serve as chair and editor in chief of Collection 15, I turned down the offer, not once, but—in the fashion of Shakespeare's *Julius Caesar*—three times. However, some gentle coaxing from our Florida Writers Association president, Mary Ann de Stefano, convinced me that our 2023 theme of secrets would be a "fun" project to work on. So, the third time turned out to be the charm, and I agreed to serve as head of the committee that worked to bring this anthology of short stories, poems, and creative nonfiction to fruition.

When submissions opened in February, I had no idea what to expect; but in just a few weeks, our membership's creative and talented writing enthralled me. As the months went on, I was honored to have the opportunity to read the heartfelt stories and poems our members submitted. By the end of April, I had read and validated over 200 entries from our adult and NextGen writers.

The pieces collected in this book only scratch the surface of what was submitted. With the most entries in the fifteen-year history of the Collection, the competition was tough, but our fine team of judges worked hard to choose what they thought the best of the submissions. As a result, readers of this anthology will have the opportunity to travel from Florida, to Paris, to Mars, and to places that only exist in the author's mind. There are stories of loves lost and found, poems of longing and joy, even a story narrated by a dog—now that's creative! But at the heart of every piece in Collection 15 there lies a secret: a secret that our esteemed members have dared to share with the world.

Before I close, I'd like to point out some changes to this year's Collection. The entries are still organized in alphabetical order by author's last name. However, our guest editor Ben Sharpton's top-ten picks are also in sequential alphabetical order, rather than at the beginning of the book, but marked with Ben's numerical ranking. Entry titles appear with the author's byline, and authors' bios and photos appear at the end of the book. Lastly, the top-five youth entries are in a separate section now referred to as NextGen Writers, since they represent the next generation of talent that will someday fill our ranks with new words and new ideas.

So now, sit back, relax, and crack open this fascinating collection of *Secrets*.

—Paul Iasevoli, Editor in Chief

Forward

by Ben Sharpton

S hhh! Do you want to know a secret? Of course, you do. Secrets are all around us. Some secrets surprise us with wonderful, unexpected delights. Others seem to impede our progress by slowing us or stopping us completely. Still others might offer pleasant diversions at otherwise mundane times.

In the literary world, writers can use secrets to spice up stories and poems to thrill readers. These secrets can make us feel afraid when they threaten us, make us feel comforted when the ground around us seems unstable, make us feel hopeful when someone who is weaker is helped, make us feel . . .. And, that's the point.

This collection is packed with secrets—stories and poems that include something unseen, untold, or hidden. One of the wonderful secrets you'll discover when you read this delightful Collection is that the poems and stories are so diverse and so well told that there is something sure to please everyone. You'll find multiple genres, diverse characters, and a variety of settings to satisfy your reading tastes. And that's a reflection of the universal writing world as well—there's enough to go around. One person may not care for one piece but another may adore it.

As I read through this well-written collection, a few that resonated with me floated to the top of my favorite list and are numerically ranked in this book. I enjoyed a poem about supporting one whose memory is fading because I lost a loved one to Alzheimer's long ago. I appreciated another about keeping our guilt over our history hidden because we all need to move beyond our past. A fantasy about secretly helping the disadvantaged among us reminded me that we do have the capacity to help others. Another story reminded me that love may be so strong it actually allows secrets to exist among partners. And some stories were simply entertaining in the way their secrets surprised and delighted me.

Take time to savor and enjoy these stories, but don't keep them a secret. Share them with others!

—Ben Sharpton, 2023 Guest Editor

An award-winning author of five novels published through independent publishers, Ben Sharpton holds three master's degrees, including an MFA in Creative Writing from Queens University. He has worked as a training and design manager with Universal Studios, Florida, and Tupperware World Headquarters and has taught college writing and business courses. Find out more at bensharpton.com.

Psiu! Hush, Hush!

By Rose Angelina Baptista

Close your eyes
to the serrating
crossing roads
of leatherback turtles
coming ashore.

Let the salty haze
quiet both the ears
and the mind which is adrift
among the salutation
of waves.

Let the breeze
billow the hairs
of your head
and brush against
your skin.

Sit
with single-pointed
concentration on the tip
of your nose or the middle
of your chest,

then
melt away
all the sea

taste
of your breath.

Your thoughts will
be traced like marine
rainbows that fade
as soon as they make
the scene.

Neither opposition nor
supposition will
snatch away
this alert
intimate seascape

full of balanced open calm,
undifferentiated beauty,
light and silky-spacious,
pious, joyful,
and pure.

My Father's Secret

by Monika Becker

U ntil the day my father called me to his hospital bed, I thought
I knew everything important about him.

"Come right away," he demanded. "I'll tell you why when you
get here." He said it in German and hung up. He insisted we speak
German, so I wouldn't forget the language.

Several years after his retirement, he began having heart trouble.
Recently, he'd passed out and ended up in the hospital. He never
called me at work, so I thought it must be serious. But he sounded
his usual strong self on the phone. What could be so pressing that
I had to leave work and come right away?

I headed for my car, thinking maybe he was told he needs surgery.
But that wouldn't scare him. He could survive most anything. Born
in Hungary, his father died when he was only six, and his mother
put him in an orphanage while she went to work. By nine, he was an
apprentice to a painter. He left his home by swimming the Danube
to get away before the Russians invaded. Years later, he managed to
get his entire family from Austria to the United States where there
were more opportunities for his children: me, an older brother, and
a younger brother.

I was seven when I ended up in a school where everyone spoke
a language I didn't understand. But our family was lucky; we had
Philipp, my older brother, who had learned English in school, so
we always had someone who could speak and read English. My
father spoke fluent German and Hungarian, but he could also make

3

himself understood in Croatian and Romanian. It didn't take him long to add English to that list.

While driving, I thought even if he were told that his condition was terminal, he wouldn't ask me to come right away. He wasn't afraid to die. "We die when the Lord wants. Our job is just to do our best," he would say.

He always did his best. We came to the United States sponsored by a limestone company. My father was contracted to dig limestone in the quarries, but he didn't stay there long. He learned the name of the company president and painted the president's name in gold Gothic script on a nameplate which he nailed to the wall where the president parked his car. The president was impressed and asked to meet the person who painted the nameplate. With his broken English, my father managed to persuade the president to give him a trial as a painter. He started out painting signs. The boss would write what was to be on the sign, and my father designed it, painted it, and told the boss what paint to order. It didn't take long before he was asked to paint everything—buildings, equipment, cranes, railroad cars, and bridges. He even got his own little building where he stored all the paint and equipment.

He became a legend at the plant. Because it took time and money to build scaffolding, he would improvise. He painted a railroad bridge while he was hanging from one arm and painting with the other. When asked to paint a boom on a large crane, he climbed to the top of the boom, put his gloved hands in paint, and slid down. When that paint dried, he repeated the procedure until the boom was painted. He could paint a room, as fast as three men, while straddling a twin-step ladder and walking it around the room with the paint can tied to the ladder. His ingenuity was not just in painting. He fixed everything around the house, and I was sure there was nothing he couldn't figure out, although he never tried to fix the TV.

As I parked the car, I thought maybe they were releasing him, and he wanted to go home right away. It didn't sound like him. He was patient and would wait until I was done with work. I remembered how we did my third-grade arithmetic problems in ink, on white linen paper evenly spaced with a ruler. He not only taught me patience, but he convinced me that girls were as smart as boys. That gave me the confidence to think I could do most anything.

When I got to his room in the hospital, he was sitting on his bed. "I want you to write down everything that I'll be doing the rest of today and all of tomorrow. I'll tell you what to write," he said, even before I said hello. "They put this monitor on me to see how my heart works."

"But they want you to write it as you're doing it so they see how your heart reacts. It's an electrocardiogram." I sat down on the chair next to his bed. I couldn't believe this was why I had to come right away.

"I told them I didn't write English, but they said they could make it out."

"You can write. You passed your driver's test and citizenship test."

"Your mother helped me memorize all that, and I talked them into letting me take those tests orally."

A nurse came in. "You must be his daughter. Just tell him he can write everything in any language he wants. We have interpreters," she said and left.

"So, just write it in German," I said.

He got agitated. "What difference does it make if I write it down after I do it or before. You write it down, and I'll do it just the way you write it. I'll tell you what to write." He handed me a pen and a sheet of paper.

I was about to argue with him but stopped. I had never thought of it before, but if he were in an orphanage at six and started his apprenticeship at nine, when did he go to school? He never talked about his childhood, and I never asked how long he was in the orphanage or if it had a school. He carefully signed his name to my report cards, but I couldn't remember him ever writing a letter. It was my mother who wrote and read all the letters that came from relatives and who read us the German magazine articles out loud each week. When important mail came, it was my brothers or I who read it first.

How, after all these years, did I never realize my father's secret? He couldn't write well enough to do this simple task. Maybe he could read enough to read traffic signs, but he didn't want anyone to know that he didn't feel confident enough in any language to write down what he did during the day. I fought back tears. He wouldn't want me to feel sorry for him. Somehow, he and my mother had managed to keep his secret. I was going to keep it too.

"You're right, Dad," I said lightly. "What difference does it make if we write it down now or later. Tell me what you want me to write."

Wedding Day

by Paula Benski

"Ooh, how about this one?" Kate squealed with delight. We were digging through my jewelry armoire looking for something she could wear at her wedding, and she had found my hidden stash of pieces in a black velvet bag at the back of the bottom drawer. Before I could stop her, she had opened the bag. In her hands was a sapphire necklace with diamonds on a white gold chain. She held it to her neck, cocking her head at her reflection in the mirror.

"Where did you get all these?" she said. "They're gorgeous, and I never see you wear them. I *love* this one."

"I inherited them from my grandmother," I said. "I don't know where she got them. Maybe at some pawn shop. You know how she liked to go to those places. Some of them look really old. I just don't feel comfortable wearing them."

"Why not?"

"I don't know. I guess I assume they all have a story and that I should know that story before I wear them." I shrugged. "I know, that sounds lame."

"No, I can see that. You always were very sensitive, Emily. It's one of the reasons I love you. I'll put it back." She reached for the velvet bag.

I never did wear any of those pieces, but I didn't feel comfortable letting her wear any of them either. I was left with the problem of finding a nice way to say no to her. I reached for the necklace and the bag to return them to their original hiding place, still pondering how best to refuse her simple request. The problem was that we had been best friends for many years, and Kate was always doing nice things for me, while it seemed I usually wasn't much of a friend back. I realized I needed to do something for her at some point. Against my better judgment, I found myself smiling at her and saying, "It *would* look beautiful with your dress."

The following Saturday was the big day. The huge reception hall was decked out to perfection with flowers everywhere. Every seat had a white rose with a name tag. The steak and lobster were beautifully prepared, and the alcohol flowed freely. It all went without a hitch.

Almost.

As Kate and Jason, the happy couple, got up to cut the cake, a shriek cut through the air. One of Jason's neighbors who had missed the wedding had just arrived at the reception, and she was pointing at Kate and screaming. No words came out of her—just a screeching sound. Jason pulled the neighbor aside and patted her arm, but she continued to point at Kate.

"You! What? You!" she sputtered at top volume, finally finding her words, and causing a big scene amongst a class of people who generally shied away from big scenes. Jason gradually steered her outside to the patio where her raised voice couldn't be heard through the heavy glass windows. I ran to be with Kate, as fast as I could in my maid-of-honor gown. She looked visibly shaken. "I'm sure it's just a misunderstanding," I said. "There can't be anything she really has against you. Does she even know you?"

Kate shook her head. "I've never met her before." She looked close to tears, and I put my arm around her and tried to soothe her. I was still holding her when Jason returned to her side.

"Can I borrow my wife for a moment, please, Emily?"

"Of course," I said. They both went out to the patio where the distraught woman was pacing. As soon as Kate stepped through the door, the woman began yelling at her. All three mouths were going, but I couldn't hear anything. It was a silent movie with my best friend stuck in a bad part.

Then the neighbor lunged at Kate, reaching for her neck, and I caught my breath. It looked like she was trying to strangle her. Jason was doing a fair job holding his neighbor back, but in a quick jab, she grabbed the necklace at Kate's throat and broke it off her neck. Kate's hands flew to her throat, and her mouth dropped open. Jason reached out to Kate, and she shook her head. He then tried to take the necklace from the woman, but she held tight to it and redirected her yelling at him. It was all I could do not to run out and deal with the woman myself. It was clear that my decision to let Kate wear the necklace was ill-advised.

The neighbor shouted at Jason for a minute or so, punctuating her tirade periodically by jabbing a finger in the air toward Kate. Then she turned and fled, still holding onto the necklace. Both Jason and Kate stared after her for a moment. You could almost see them think through the benefits of running after her versus returning to the cake-cutting ceremony before the rest of the guests got restless. Jason put an arm around Kate and steered her back into the hall. They smiled for the guests, provided a plausible explanation for the drama that was just displayed for everyone, then proceeded to cut the cake. Afterward, Kate pulled me aside to fill me in.

"Oh Emily, I'm so sorry! That awful woman insisted your necklace had belonged to her sister who was murdered a few years ago. She broke it off my neck and ran off with it." She relayed this information as if I hadn't seen it through the windows with everyone else.

"Of course, she is mistaken," she continued. "I *will* get it back. I'm so sorry."

"Don't worry about it," I said, patting her on the shoulder as I had just seen Jason do.

"But that's not fair to you, Emily. We have to get that necklace back."

I took a deep breath. "Maybe not. Remember that it *could* be her sister's necklace." *It is.* "Maybe from a pawn shop, remember?" *But that's not how I got it.* "Don't worry about it." *Please drop it.*

I knew I should have protected all that jewelry better—but I got careless. I let a friendship lead me into a bad decision. So now here I am again, looking over my previously hidden collection—one piece for each target I have killed. They have all given me great joy, but the risks are too high now. I must dispose of them all.

A Secret Is . . .

by Nancy Lee Bethea

A hidden morsel,
Of Truth or Lie.
Dormant
Until it benefits
Its owner
To tell it,
Or sell it,
Or quell it,
Or yell it,
Or swell with pride
At possessing such a
Delectable crumb
From
The cake of knowledge.

Mangar the Armored One

by P. K. Brent

"I'm not going inside!" Jay insisted. "You can't make me."

"Me neither. I'm staying out all night," Tom added.

Lucy, the babysitter, pondered the situation, a full mutiny on her hands and a miserable night looming ahead.

"Fine with me if you two stay out all night. I don't care. Your mother won't be home until tomorrow afternoon, so she'll never know."

"You won't tell on us?"

"Of course not. I wouldn't want your mom to think I can't handle things. But I'm not staying outside with you. I must be extra careful after what happened to my brother's best friend, Frank."

"What happened to Frank?"

"It's a secret. I shouldn't say."

"We won't tell!"

"Promise?"

"Yes! Tell us, Lucy. Please tell us."

"Okay. But you can't tell anyone. Yet you need to know, so you can be on the lookout. You both must promise not to spill this secret. If people found out, the real estate values in this neighborhood would tank. Our parents would lose a lot of money. No more soccer camps and video games for you. No more college for me."

Both boys solemnly nodded.

"I'm not crazy. I know I'm not crazy because I heard everything from my window, and my brother filled in the details. I peeked, but at first didn't understand what was happening. It was so dark and terrible . . . what happened to Frank. You might think this story is

11

crazy, but it's entirely true. I will tell you about a monster called Magnar the Armored One."

"Magnar? That name sounds scary."

"Magnar is scary! He's huge and armored. His snout is pointed, like a sword. His mouth is full of sharp teeth. But before he bites, Magnar swirls his long, pink tongue all over his victim's face. Magnar is feared throughout the forest."

The boys looked at each other, concerned.

"You know how our yards back up to that nature trail?"

"Yes?"

"You know how that nature trail leads to the Ocala National Forest, which has thousands of wild, wooded acres and ravines?"

"Yes."

"At the bottom of the deepest ravine, in a cave, lives Magnar the Armored One. I know all about Magnar, but knowing will do me no good. The regular monsters are bad enough, but Magnar is the worst. You hear that? That noise is Magnar the Armored One coming down the trail toward us, looking for me."

Tom gasped, as they heard a sound in the brush from far down the nature trail.

"It's nothing! Just the wind," said Jay.

"You'll be wishing it was just the wind. The tramping is getting louder now. Listen, and you will hear it start and then stop. Magnar is stalking me. He's covered in scales and looks prehistoric, like a dinosaur. His claws are long; his snout is long. Magnar sounds like a small tank when he moves. His fortress of scales is impregnable. No one can stop him once he decides to do mayhem. He did mayhem on Frank, poor kid. Frank was covered with cuts from sharp claws when they found him unconscious on the lawn. His mouth was full of black dirt. Worms and grubs squirmed out. Frank was never the same again. He is marked by scars all over his body, and his mind is shattered. Frank was so scared that his family had to move away."

The noise on the trail was now undeniable and moving closer. Tom sat up. Even Jay stopped to listen. *Tramp! Tramp! Tramp!* sounded through the underbrush.

"Magnar is moving down the trail in our direction. He's not fast, due to his size. He rests, but he never stops. When he attacked Frank, he saw me watching from a window. I can still hear Frank's blood-curdling screams. Magnar is after me now. He doesn't like to leave witnesses. He'll take anyone he finds with me. You hear him? It would take a monster the size of a car to make that much racket. We're not safe here. I'm not safe anywhere, but I know enough to hide and turn off the lights. No one is safe sitting outside with me around."

"I'll be right back." Lucy returned after turning off all the lights inside and outside the house. The boys squirmed nervously in the dark.

"Some kids say Frank ran away. Others say his father is a secret agent, and his family joined the Witness Protection Program, then moved to Arizona. I know the truth because I saw what happened in the dusk from my window. I saw the claw marks all over Frank. I heard the screams. It's a miracle Magnar let Frank live. No one believed Frank when he said what happened. That's why he went crazy. No one would believe me now, but you can hear Magnar drawing closer."

The noise was closer. Louder. It now sounded like a small tank slowly rolling through the underbrush—starting, then stopping, then starting again. Both boys changed chairs to sit closer to the door.

"Back when Frank got hurt, I heard this same tramping noise on the trail for weeks after. I knew it was Magnar looking for more victims, looking for me. I told my friend, Sarah, next door, not to leave her cat out all night. Sarah didn't believe me. She didn't listen. Magnar the Armored One ate Snickers. All Sarah could find when she called Snickers the next morning was a pile of little bones and a tiny skull. Cat bones! Magnar spit the bones on Sarah's back porch to rub it in and make her feel worse."

Tom whimpered and even Jay looked nervous. The tramping noise along the trail could not be denied. It was now a loud racket. Both boys stood by the door, Tom gripping the handle tightly. Lucy spoke only in a whisper.

"My situation is hopeless. It gets easier to accept what will happen when you admit the truth. I'm doomed. I can smell doom in the air. One of these nights, Magnar will get me. I'll be taking the trash out or calling the dog in, and Magnar will be waiting. But I'm determined to last as long as I can. I'll make it to college. I won't do anything stupid on purpose, so I'm going inside now before Magnar finds me. When you start screaming, don't expect me to save you."

A branch cracked loud and close by. Tom swung the door open, and both boys ran fast inside, down the hall, and to their bedroom, without turning on a light.

Lucy grinned. In the shadows, she could see a little armadillo enter the yard with his scales, claws, and long snout. A moment later, he began digging for worms.

Gallery of Secrets

by William Clapper

"I'm done. I can't stand having him around anymore." Maddie tossed her leather bag on the bar. "Liz, I'll do anything to get rid of him."

Liz saw red streaks of anger in Maddie's aura. "You know, he's not going to change," she said, rimming Maddie's Hendricks and tonic with lime. "Maybe it's time for you to make some changes."

Maddie swirled the ice in her drink. "You're right. His shirt reeked of perfume this morning. What's he doing? Hookers? One-night stands?"

Liz knew Maddie's marriage was in tatters thanks to their frequent afternoon conversations. She braced against the bar's back counter. "Sounds like he's doin' you wrong, girlfrien'. Where's he work? Maybe he's got something on the side."

"A work slut? Nah. He doesn't have an office. Or a regular job. He never talks about work. I never ask, because I don't want to know."

Liz pulled at her left ear. "That doesn't say much for your relationship."

"He said it's better that I don't know what he does and not to ask him again." Maddie leaned toward Liz and whispered, "He's gone for days and then shows up with a roll of cash. I think he's into drugs or something, you know?"

Maddie's anger ruffled the dark hairs on Liz's forearms. "There are ways to get him out of your life." Liz's bartender voice carried no farther than their shared space. "Catch him cheating. File for divorce. Go to the cops. Or, you could pack up and leave. You've got no kids. No complications."

"I'm not leaving and giving up my life here." Maddie cradled her drink; her rings clicked against the glass. "My parents left me the house. It's all mine."

Liz stretched her arms overhead, then tugged on the hem of her black shirt to cover her exposed belly. "Has he ever hit you?"

"He's threatened, but he's never hit me. Thank God." The venom left her voice. "I just want him to disappear. Get out of my life. He's verbally abusive; he ignores me. He makes fun of my art. And it's getting worse."

Liz scanned the empty bar and dining area. "Maddie, we're friends. I can trust you with a secret way to deal with someone like him. But you must be strong and committed to handle the consequences."

Maddie's sea-gray eyes widened, and her mouth opened a notch. "What are you saying?

Liz held a beer glass to the overhead light, looking for water spots. "What I'm saying is there are ways to get your husband out of your life, if that's what you want."

Two lumps of ice and the lime wedge puddled in the bottom of Maddie's glass. "Divorce is messy, and he'd fight me all the way. He lashes out when he's mad. I couldn't prove he's into something, so the cops would do nothing." She caressed the malachite at her sternum. "You say there are other ways? Let me think on that. I'll let you know"

Maddie weaved around the few occupied tables, trailed by a tall, thin man—his swarthy face inclined to his phone. She waved to Liz and headed for a small table tucked into an alcove.

"So, this is Liz's Secret Bar." He swept the bar area and the two occupied tables in the dining area. "You gotta be kidding. I'm not having dinner in this dump."

"C'mon, Artie. The food's good, and I want you to meet my friend Liz." Maddie averted her attention to the menu. "You said you would be nice. And I deserve a little bit of consideration after this afternoon."

Artie hunched forward. "You deserve what? Listen, you pissed me off; I was upset, and I lost control. I said I was sorry. Get over it."

Liz pushed through a cloud of tension and anger as she approached the table. She heard most of what Artie said and fixed her gaze on Maddie. "What can I get you guys to drink?"

"Gin and tonic for me." Liz felt the edge in her friend's voice. "By the way, this is my husband, Artie."

"Hello, Artie. What can I getcha?"

Artie interrupted his screen swiping to visually measure Liz's ample upper torso. "Fetch me a Jack, neat."

She was a fraction of a second too slow to avoid Artie's pat on her hip. She shifted and leaned into the space between herself and Artie. "None of that in this bar."

"Hey, don't get your panties in a knot. I'm only trying to be friendly."

"My panties are fine. Do that again, and you'll be out of here."

"Yeah, yeah. Just get my drink." The phone beckoned, and Artie resumed swiping.

She turned to Maddie. "How you been? Haven't seen you in a while. Everything okay?" A faint purple bruise on Maddie's upper arm and discoloration along her right cheek that make-up couldn't obscure caught Liz's attention. *Bastard.* Liz's eyes darted to Artie and back. She raised an eyebrow to her friend.

Maddie twitched in her seat. "Yeah. I'm fine." She curled a tendril of hair between her fingers. "You know, Liz, there are many ways to deal with things. And I'm dealing."

Liz ambled back behind the bar to fix their drinks. "Don't get close to that guy. He's got roving hands," she told her server. "Take their order, and don't hover."

After the other diners were gone and the table was cleared, Liz came over to Maddie's table with their check. "Thanks for coming in tonight. Hope everything was okay."

"Yeah, great," Artie grunted. He tossed three twenties on the table. "Keep the change, babe."

Liz retrieved the bills and gathered the empty dessert plates. "Would you guys mind me taking your picture?" She motioned toward a far wall. "I've started a customer photo gallery."

Maddie nodded her okay and glanced at an antique camera Liz carried.

Liz led them to the gallery. "This old camera's wonky. So, Maddie, would you take a practice shot? Here's the eyepiece. When you're ready, push this button. I'll put my hand on your shoulder to steady you."

Maddie sighted the bulky Graflex, and a yellow light bathed Artie when she tripped the shutter. Artie faded away, as Maddie stared at his image coalescing on the camera's glass focus plate.

Panic flashed in her eyes. "Where did he go? Liz, what have I done?"

"That's the secret of getting rid of your husband, Maddie."

"Will he come back? Or is he, you know, dead?"

"Not dead. He's suspended in a place where he can't hurt you. He's there forever, or until you want to bring him back. His photograph will make a nice addition to my gallery."

"You mean he's trapped in the picture forever? What am I going to do?"

"Prepare a good story. You've got to get yourself together and make a plan before people start looking for him. I'll help you with that." Liz sensed a tremor of relief surge through Maddie.

"Give me a couple of days to think this through. We need to talk. And thanks, for everything."

Liz took the camera, and her eyes bored into Maddie. "No worries. Girlfriends have secrets."

An Unshared Memory

by Scott Corey

In my grandfather's bedroom was a closet with an old, yellow door and an ornate metal doorknob worn smooth by years of turning. The closet was in the corner of the bedroom beside his bed, and I was not allowed to look in there except by permission. On those occasions when I was allowed to turn the smooth knob, feeling big in my hands and mysterious in anticipation, the door would open, and I would be struck by the smell of moth balls, old flannel shirts, trousers worn shiny on the creases with ironing, and leather shoes polished to the softness of an old harness.

It was not just idle curiosity that prompted me to open the door. There were many closets in my grandparent's house, but this was the only one that caught my imagination. For in this closet, set deep in a corner and hidden behind a faded robe, was my grandpa's old hunting rifle. It was a small rifle, with a heavy barrel, and worn stock; but to me it was an artifact of the Civil War, of Davy Crockett, of the Colonial Militia and their fight against the British, of a lone frontier scout slipping silently through the deep forests of the past in search of the mysterious land beyond. All these thoughts came to me when I ran my fingers over the smooth stock, and I could imagine myself in all of those places. I was that frontier scout; I had walked sentry duty through the snow at Valley Forge; and I had paddled up the Missouri river with Lewis and Clark.

When I asked Grandpa if I could shoot the rifle, he touched his hand to the barrel thoughtfully and said no, that the old gun no longer worked. The last time he had tried to fire it—many years ago—the hammer had broken off and blown back past his ear. He only kept it around now for the memories.

I wondered what memories he had of the gun, and if they were like mine, but we never discussed it. He would only sit there with me on his bed and look at the rifle for a few minutes and then, gazing off distantly, say it was time to put the old gun away. I would set it awkwardly back in the corner, for it was heavy, cover it over again with the faded robe, and close the door. Then I would go outside and pick up a stick or piece of wood and run through the forests of my imagination, even though I was only in the backyard of a small Indiana town.

I don't know whatever happened to the rifle. I know that once, when I was a teenager, I broke the rules and opened the closet door without asking, but the rifle wasn't there. When I inquired about it later, my father told me the rifle had been given to my grandfather by his father. This made me wonder, because I knew my grandfather's mother died when he was nine years old, and he had been sent to live in a series of foster homes. My grandfather had a difficult childhood. Yet the rifle always remained with him.

I wondered if, instead of colonial forests and battles, my grandfather's imagination had taken him back to an earlier time, when he was a boy too and had spent time with his father. Those would have been precious memories for him, and I can better understand now the distant gaze that came into his eyes as we sat together on the bed. Naturally, he would have wanted to put the rifle away after a few minutes, for some memories cannot be shared—even with a boy who gazed at his tennis shoes and saw moccasins.

Nasty

by Lynda Courtright

Winter sunshine sifts through the lace curtains of Nora's west-facing windows, spilling golden light on the oriental rug and the cold tile around it. Nora has turned on the heater, and it's finally taken the chill out of the air. We all moved to Florida to stay warm, but here we are, huddled around Nora's table nibbling brownies warm from her oven, glad we didn't send all our northern clothes to Goodwill.

We are the Eagleshore Ladies' Canasta Group, or the E.L.C.G., for short. We meet Tuesday afternoons at the Eagleshore Apartment building to play cards in the apartment of whoever is host that week. Nora and Ruthie and I started the E.L.C.G. five years ago. Charlotte joined us a little later when she moved to Florida. We've walked one another through a divorce (Nora's), a husband's death (my Scott), and chemo for Ruthie and Charlotte.

This week, we found out that Ruthie's leaving us. She's moving into assisted living for the usual reasons: forgetting her meds, a couple of falls, and melting a pan on her stove. Her daughter Gina came to visit at Christmas and immediately began looking for a place in Pittsburgh near where she lives. Ruthie has made up her mind to go but is still trying to find someone to take her dog before Gina arrives tomorrow to pack her up.

There are four of us playing cards today. We invited Grace, the new lady who moved in on the second floor, to fill in for Ruthie. Nora and Charlotte and I think Grace will be a good replacement for our departing friend, and we hope she likes our group. Not only does she know how to play canasta, which is almost a lost skill these days, but she can teach us bridge and mahjong.

We've finished three hands of canasta so far. I begin dealing the fourth and final hand, card by card, *slap, slap, slap* on the table until each player has eleven. The remainder of the deck goes in the middle of the table, and the top card is turned up. My partner today is Nora, and we're ahead after the three hands, 4,220 to 3,915. Everyone picks up their cards and arranges them how they like, stealing sly glances at their partners to glean clues from facial expressions. Of course, after you play canasta with the same people for this many years, you can practically read your partner's mind, but so can rival players. Like poker, it's a game of tricks and deceit.

I miss Ruthie already. But one good thing about her leaving is we won't have to worry anymore about the manager discovering her dog. The Eagleshore is a no-pets-allowed apartment building and, for all these years, our Ruthie has cleverly kept management's eye off her dog, Molly. Other than the four of us, I don't think any other tenants know Molly's here, which is remarkable. Up till Ruthie's fall a month ago, she walked Molly in the park across the street three times a day.

Molly is a Maltese poodle, so small she'd fit in your hands. She looks like a tiny Ewok, with long, soft brown-and-gray fur and great big eyes. Ruthie used to carry her in one of those reusable shopping bags that have handles on top. She kept the bag half full of yarn, the same colors as Molly's fur. Before the elevator door would open to let Ruthie and Molly on, Ruthie would say, "Nighty-night!" That was the command for Molly to duck down in the yarn and stay very still. If people on the elevator asked what was in the bag, Ruthie said she had taken up crocheting. No one in the world imagined Ruthie would put one over on them. Meanwhile, Molly would snuggle safely in the yarn until Ruthie said, "Hello!" which was the signal that she could poke her head back out the top of the bag.

It's my turn to play. I take the discard pile because there's a jack on top of it, and I have four jacks in my hand. I lay five jacks and two wild cards on the table, giving Nora and me a mixed canasta worth 300 points, and putting us on the board. I sneak a look at Nora to see if she is proud of me. But, although I'm not sure, I think she looks disappointed. Was she collecting jacks too? I sigh and roll my eyes. She shrugs and rearranges the cards in her hand.

Ruthie has invited us to come to her apartment after we get done playing. She wants each of us to take something to remember her by. She asked her son Joel if he will take Molly, but she hasn't heard back. He's always so busy. Molly is Ruthie's biggest worry now. Gina has declined. She has dogs, a job, and three children. "Get information from the Humane Society" is her advice. "Molly's cute; someone will adopt her."

"No one loves an old dog," says Ruthie. Molly's been Ruthie's most faithful companion for a long time. Nora says Ruthie even lets Molly sleep in bed with her, which I think is disgusting. Nasty, when you know Molly has accidents sometimes and farts a lot.

Nora has discarded two jacks and laid down four aces: the beginnings of a straight canasta, which she doesn't know yet, because I'm holding the three aces in my hand. I work hard not to look excited, but can't resist glancing at her. She's deadpan. Much better than I am at concealing anything.

It's Grace's turn. She announces that she's going out. The game is over. I'm holding the aces and jokers. Grace and Charlotte win.

Did I reveal my position to Grace? I'm embarrassed to ask, so I don't. It's all in fun anyway, isn't it?

We pack up the cards and take the brownie plate back to the kitchen. Nora transfers four brownies to a plastic bag for Ruthie to share with her daughter tomorrow. Grace declines the stop at Ruthie's since she's only met her once, but she promises to play cards with us next Tuesday.

We three old friends ride the elevator silently to the sixth floor. The bell dings, the door opens, and I remember giggling with Ruthie as we took her little secret in a bag of yarn to the park. We step out, carrying greeting cards and a framed photo of the four of us sitting at Nora's table. Ruthie has left the door open, so we go right in.

Nora chooses porcelain teacups and saucers hand painted in 1918 by someone who signed her name Inez. Charlotte picks three books from Ruthie's shelves.

I sign my name in the dusty buffet. "I don't know what to take. But I'll never forget you."

Ruthie's eyes twinkle. "I believe you." She nods toward the door.

The bag of yarn sits there. I passed right by it coming in. "Is that empty, or—?" *Never, never in my bed*, I say to myself.

Ruthie smiles. "Hello!"

I Will Be Your Memory #1

by Jennifer Reed Cox

Is Jennifer coming? Yes, I tell you
though I am Jennifer
I imagine shaking you until my smart, sly mother falls out

She's in there. She still sings all the words of the old hymns,
toe tapping out the promise of an unbroken circle,
remembered
with Granddaddy at the all-night gospel sings,
in Montgomery under a tent,
remembered

But where you sleep or who I am
do you have a toothbrush, and where's Daddy?
These things live in the sinkholes of your grey matter
so the doctors say, not gone
just difficult to access

A CT image is black, vacant, where it should be white
dark where the memories hide
the calendar that dictated life before
now is a puzzle you cannot solve

we laugh and we go on and we pretend
that this shell is my mother
You escape occasionally
maneuvering around the empty spaces

When our gazes hold—yours in mine in yours
You are there, for me

Your hand in mine in yours
Your hand IS mine IS yours
The arthritic arch of our little fingers twinned
in our twined hands

Thank you for trying so hard to be present today
this moment,
faking remembrance so well
in return I will pretend that
I don't know that you don't know

Unearthing Dozier's Dirt

by Melody Dean Dimick

Who will expose
the one-armed man swinging,
beating with the leather strap, staining
flannel pajamas with maroon blood?

Orphan boys' blood on the walls,
grinding of the old fan while bed
springs sing the poor boy's blues.
Did you look the other way, Good Rector?

Who will expose
the one-armed man whipping, whipping,
avenging his own lifelong cross?
What did you see, Good Rector?

Holes behind the chow hall
four-feet deep and as long as a boy—
child buried under white, wooden cross
waiting, waiting to be uncovered.

To put food on the table
for your children, did you look
the other way while my grandson died?
Could it be possible, Good Rector?

Did you know the blood of fifty-five
innocent children stained the hands

that signed your paychecks, man of God?
Did you sell your soul to the devil?

Were you too weak to stand up
for good when tempted by evil?
Did you pen lies?
Were you there when my grandson

was forced to write,
"I got what was coming to me?"
Do you pray with the hands that typed
the dishonest letter you signed?

When anthropologists from the university
lifted shovels, unearthed, and exposed
bodies behind the chow hall,
how did you have the audacity to pray?

Like the *Mona Lisa*, you're quite an enigma.
Pray, tell me your secrets, Good Rector.

The Old Chair

by Lynda R. Edwards

They were exhausted. They had been cleaning and organizing for nearly six hours. It was astounding to Brian and Angie that they knew nothing relevant about the old couple's lives. They were neighbors for nearly fifteen years and close, or so Brian and Angie thought.

"They never mentioned any family?" Brian asked, as he went through the papers on the old man's desk.

"Brian, how many times do I have to answer the same question?" Angie replied, exasperated. "I know they had no children, but neither of them mentioned any family."

"No brothers or sisters?" Brian continued, baffled. "No nieces or nephews?"

Angie ignored him. She didn't know the answers to the questions a month ago when the police knocked at the door asking if they knew the couple who died next door. She didn't know the answers to the questions the police asked her about whom they should contact. She didn't understand why she and Brian were willed the house when a lawyer contacted them after the couple's death.

Over the years, the old woman had helped her through some difficult times. She took Angie to her first AA meeting, when Angie's drinking was too much for her to overcome alone.

The old man invited Brian over, and they sat by the pool, sometimes talking but mostly just sitting, while Brian brooded. Brian wasn't much of a talker. Neither was the old man. When Brian was leaving, the old man put his hand on Brian's shoulder. "All marriages have their ups and downs. The thing to remember is why you fell in love with her."

"She makes it so hard sometimes," the admission escaping Brian before he could stop himself.

"That's why it's important to remember," the old man said softly. "So you can fall in love with her all over again. This will pass, and you'll both be better off going through it together because it won't be the last one. Something else will come along. It always does."

And it had. Angie's sobriety was something Brian was proud of. But he couldn't help the feelings of anger and resentment that flared up later.

"I don't know what to do," Angie cried to the old woman. "He's angry and distant. Being with him is so hard when he's like this."

"Love him through it. He's feeling the fear he denied himself when you were fighting your demons," the old woman advised. "He'll return to you when he understands your love isn't going anywhere."

And he had. Now they worked through the office, packing away things they didn't know the value of. A life lived revealed in snapshots, Post-it notes, insurance policies, and legal documents.

"I just don't understand why they left everything to us," Brian said again, more baffled than anything else.

"Brian, for the hundredth time, I don't know!" Angie replied.

But we should have known, they both thought guiltily.

They were going through another rough patch. The distance between them seemed to be a chasm too wide to traverse. Their marriage didn't need the stress of unraveling the mystery the old couple left them. It took a lot of work to close the book on a life lived for decades, and Angie wasn't sure her marriage would survive the task.

"Wow, look at this!" Brian exclaimed.

"What is it?" Angie asked.

"A box filled with letters," Brian said, pulling a large, ornate, wooden box from behind the desk. "But they've never been opened."

Angie took a pile of letters secured by a rubber band from him. He held another pile in his hand.

"They're addressed to each of them," Angie said, looking from her pile to his. "From him to her and her to him."

"They wrote letters to each other but never read them?" Brian asked, surprised.

Brian and Angie looked at each other. Did they dare? "Maybe they have some of the answers we're looking for," Angie offered.

She sat in the overstuffed, brown chair next to the desk. Brian sat at the desk. They started reading.

"She suffered another miscarriage," Angie said, pain in her voice.

"What's the date of that letter?" Brian asked.

"January fourth, 1982," Angie answered.

"It was her third miscarriage," Brian said, looking up from the letter he held.

They glanced at each other.

"He wanted to leave," Brian said halfway through another letter. "July fifteenth, 1986."

Angie looked at the date on the letter she pulled from the pile. "She knew. What does he say?"

"That he's sorry," Brian summarized. "He was devastated after learning they couldn't have children. She pulled away from him, and he didn't know what to do."

"She felt she failed him," Angie replied, scanning a letter she held. "She couldn't give him the one thing she knew he wanted—the family neither of them had growing up."

"He says she was the only family he ever wanted," Brian whispered. "But he didn't know how to comfort her or to make her realize how much he loved her. He thought he'd lost her."

"She recognized that her regret was a wedge between them," Angie replied, tears in her eyes.

"They bought this house," Brian continued. "They wanted a fresh start. A dedication to their love and recommitment to the marriage."

"This chair was the first thing they bought for the house," Angie sighed. "They put it next to his desk, so she could be with him."

"She kissed me, sat in her chair, and all was right in my world," Brian read from a letter.

"They met us!" Angie read.

Brian grabbed another letter. He remembered they met the old couple in 2002, when he and Angie moved in next door.

"He says that I love you as much as he loved her. He recognizes it in the way I look at you," Brain said.

"She says the same about me," Angie replied softly.

They gazed at each other. Angie sat in the chair she had seen the old woman sitting in as her husband worked. Brian remembered the old woman's tinkle of laughter as the old man said something amusing while he sat at the desk, smiling at her. Angie stared at the chair, running her hand along the plush arm. She looked up at Brian as his hand met hers.

The letters contained everything the old couple had left unsaid. They wrote about things that needed to be released but not revealed and left them behind in unopened envelopes. By freeing themselves of the past, they found their way back to each other in a love story that not even death could bring an end to, and the old chair witnessed it all.

The last letter was addressed to Brian and Angie:

> If you are reading this, then you know we see you in ourselves. Learn from our mistakes, because we lived an extraordinary life together. We were meant to love each other, just as you are; so trust us when we promise you, it will be the greatest love you will ever know and worth every minute you invest in each other. That's the secret to true love; it weathers every storm to find a safe harbor.

Island Girl

by Elena Fowler

I'm an island girl,
from my toes to my very soul.
I breathe in the summer breezes
that spin and break upon sparkling blue waters.

Cradled by the gentle sea
I hold fast my secret, my run away longing to join
those long-haired mermaids and their fast-flying dolphins.

And when I see my island people smile,
I feel the weathered beats of their hearts spill with kindness,
as though the summer rains have never fallen upon their souls.

Sharing their laughter with the fading warmth of a blazing sun,
their world is filled with bold sunset colors that streak
sea-stained blues and seaweed greens and even, hot lipstick pinks.

For me it matters not the island or its compass point,
but the strong love we share,
for the sea that gathers us up and marks us as her own.

Is it this heat that slowly drums and dulls our senses,
making us content with the daily rhythms of sea, salt, and wind?
Or could it be something deeper these sandy feet cannot fathom,
clinging to my heart, this touch of wet blue home?

Rough bits of sand play upon my cotton sheets,
tempting me to remember shades of unity
within this soul: life, death, and rebirth.
Faithfully bringing me back to stand before this wanting sea?

I claim all islands,
as a place I lay my head and heart,
for I soulfully love the rhythm of an island life.

So when you see me out upon its seas,
know I close my eyes and ride with trust.
Happy to be free and gliding upon the mounting curl,
of a heated crashing wave.

For I am at home with my long-haired mermaids,
playing among those fast-flying dolphins of the sea,
with a heart that beats fierce, true, and wet.

The Most Prized Possession

by Lorrie Gault

George and his new pal Andy sat on the front porch of George's farmhouse, sipping cheap beer, and rocking their chairs in squeaky rhythm. Failing eyesight prevented the octogenarians from seeing much beyond the porch steps, but George was positive he'd know when his felon grandson, Nate, showed up. Didn't matter that he hadn't been by for the past two years because he was "cooped up in the can," as George liked to say. Some things never changed. He'd squeal the tires and lay on the horn before bolting up the steps three at a time, same as always. Today, Nate was getting out, and George expected a visit shortly.

"Nate was never what you'd call a rocket scientist," George was telling Andy. "Lived down in Roseville all his unproductive twenty-four years. Still, he'd kept his nose clean up till the Gus Rogers incident here in Huntstown. That one was a doozie, though. Much as I love that boy, he's a mutton head, and tellin' him Gus's secret after all this time will prove it."

"Understandable, your frustration, bein' a retired marine an' all," said Andy, who took careful aim and spit over the side of the porch rail. "What'd he do?"

"Dang fool. Always lookin' for a quick way to make a buck without exertin' an ounce of respectable effort." George shook his head and popped the top on another lager. "His daddy visited him in prison. Not my idea. I thought he should toughen up, be on his own inside. Get the crap scared outta him, so he'd never do nothin' like that again. But he begged his daddy. Said he'd tell him everything, if he'd come see him regular and, a course, then his daddy told me. Gus filled in the gaps. It happened like this . . ."

———

Nate roared into Huntstown on the pretense of visiting his grandfather. He needed cash fast and decided to take a quick look-see around town for an easy mark, make his move, and then a quick exit. If he needed an alibi, his grandfather would be perfect. George had been a well-respected citizen of Huntstown forever.

It didn't take long to find the perfect target: Gus Rogers's Antiques and Fine Used Furniture Emporium—cluttered with heaps of heistable doodads. After a short visit with Grandpa, Nate cased the place, feigning interest in an oriental rug. His true focus, however, was on a fancy box that Gus had displayed on a gleaming Edwardian étagère.

Nate hastily hatched a dimwit plan: swipe the box and pawn it without ado the next state over. Heck, Gus probably wouldn't even miss it. Similar boxes were strewn around the shop in the tangle of merchandise piled to the rafters. But this particular box was more ornate, with lots of jewels and such. Yeah, it'd fetch a hefty price.

Nate pocketed a Hellcat pistol with the serial number filed off, borrowed from a high school dropout buddy, just in case, and made his move. Although heavier than he'd expected, he snatched the box, clumsily shoved it under his army surplus jacket, and strode out the front door without a backward glance. Neglecting to keep his eye on the owner, he never noticed that Gus spotted the missing box straight away. Gus whipped out his phone and called the cops post haste, before he lit off after the bandit without a second thought.

Nate heard sirens and panicked. Slight change in plans. He spun his tires, leaving a trail of thick dust behind, and detoured to Grandpa's house where he hastily wrapped the box in a Winn Dixie bag dug out from under the driver's seat and implored George to "keep something" for him for a hot minute. He'd be back soon.

He made it just sixty yards around the corner before crashing smack dab into Gus's F-150, blew a tire, then tried running away with a gimpy leg. Gus, frantic and shaking with rage, was not to be deterred. He caught up with Nate and took him down like a roped calf. By then, the entire Huntstown police force had flocked to the scene. Nate was toast. Even as a first offender, carrying an illegal weapon guaranteed him a stiff prison sentence.

Sure enough, at five p.m., George and Andy heard a squeal, a honk, and the thuds of running footsteps.

"I finally made it back, Grandpop," Nate yelled without preamble, as he mounted the porch steps three at a time. He slapped George a little too hard on the shoulder in greeting. Close up, George could see Nate hadn't changed much. Wiry now, though, and in need of a proper haircut and shave.

"I've been waitin' years for this," Nate said. "I paid my dues, and I'm ready to reclaim that package what's rightfully mine." He danced from foot to foot in anticipation. "Better late than never, yeah?"

George sighed. He'd had hopes for the boy, but the crazy kid was no smarter now than when they hauled him away in cuffs.

"So, your daddy never did tell you, huh?"

"Tell me what?"

"Gus and me been friends a bear's age." George paused and fiddled with his beer can. "I gave the box back to him, Nate. Right away. Before they even threw you in the slammer."

"You did what?" Nate shook his head in clear disbelief. "But we're kin. I was countin' on you, Grandpop. All that miserable time in the joint I dreamt of collectin' my stuff and startin' over. Now you're tellin' me you gave it back?"

"Wasn't no reason to keep it," George said, his disappointment hard to miss, even for Andy, who was squinting back and forth at George and Nate like Mr. Magoo.

Nate plopped down on the top step, breathless, as though dropped by a Mike Tyson left. For a moment, only an obnoxious crow mouthing off overhead broke the silence.

"You blew it, boy. You earned yourself a ticket to prison for nothin'."

"What do you mean? Rogers told everybody who looked at that box, 'This is my most prized possession.' Like a goddamn parrot. That's why I pinched it. How'd I know he'd lose his flippin' mind over it and track me down? Come on, Grandpop. It has to be worth a lot."

"Nope, sorry son. Not to nobody but Gus. He bought that box at a flea market back in '82 for twelve bucks because Vera, his wife of forty years, thought it was beautiful. Didn't matter to her that the wood was just veneer, and the jewels were paste. Heck, even the latch was imitation ivory."

George leaned forward, hands on knees, and stared straight into Nate's defeated, blue eyes. "You see, boy, Vera passed away a month before you showed up in town. And that box you wanted so bad? It held Vera's dear, departed ashes."

Yard Work

by Carolyn Greeley

"Damn! I hate yardwork." She straightened, using the metal rake to support herself, and eased into a stretch. "This sucks." She rubbed her lower back. The shooting pain abated but left a dull throb that resisted her ministrations. "This isn't a yard, though. Yards are for normal people. This is a jungle. I hate jungle work." She turned at the sound of her husband's approach.

"If you hate it, why do you keep doing it?" He set down the clippers, came around behind her, and began massaging—dirt-covered hands leaving smudges on her light-blue T-shirt. She didn't mind.

"Lower." She dropped her head, leaning forward as he complied. "Because I love you, and I'm trying to help, so you don't have to do *all* the work." The words sounded muffled, as she spoke to her chest. "And because it's partly my responsibility. We bought this crazy place, and those druggies never did anything good here, inside, or out. So, we have to clean everything, including, occasionally, this jungle."

He rested his hands on her shoulders and turned her. "You're pretty cool, you know?" She smiled, and he shook her lightly. "But don't overdo it. Take a break if you need to."

"I will. I just want to finish this section. Remember what a beast this was? All those overgrown azaleas and saw palmettos? Now look. It's fabulous!" She waved her arm to encompass a sun-spattered, ten-by-twenty-foot portion of their backyard that she'd liberated. "You can almost see the fence." Then she made a face. "It's these friggin' vines that are the worst! Raking out all this debris and the cuttings . . . I feel like the vines are trying to suck me into the green."

"I know. But this looks great."

"I have that last area under there to clear out, then I'll stop."

He replied with a shrug and a head shake, then grabbed the hedge clippers and turned away.

Slightly refreshed, she inhaled the humid Florida air, gritted her teeth, and tromped into the fray. "Die, vines, die."

The final patch burrowed beneath a live oak weeping Spanish moss and the thicket of azaleas she'd saved to soften the scenery. She launched the rake into the bushes and tugged with all her remaining effort. A swath of vines and weeds broke loose, and she staggered backward. "Almost got it."

She dragged the weeds out and dove back in. "C'mon, you sonofa . . .." Again, she yanked the rake through the underbrush, clearing until a furrow of loamy-smelling, chocolate-colored soil remained. "Got you, you bastard." With one final heave, she thunked the rake into the dirt. A loud clank jostled the air. "Ugh, another brick," she muttered, as she inched forward to clear out the rubbish.

Squatting, she peered at the earth in the shadow of the azalea shrub. She used the rake to poke around the dirt and uncover what she'd clunked into. When that proved unwieldy, and the item not a brick, she retrieved a trowel from their excuse of a shed and began to dig.

The top of a rust-splotched metal container appeared, dull silver glinting in the spots where the rake had gouged the surface. She scraped through the dirt around the box to uncover the edges, measuring about six inches by twelve. A hinged, oblong ring appeared on the lid. She tugged gently, trying to free the case without opening it, but the box didn't budge. Digging deeper, she freed part of the bottom section, about four inches down, and levered the hand spade underneath to pry the container loose.

The metal case sprang out, lighter than she expected, and she rocked back on her heels. "Babe," she called across the yard. She waved an arm to flag him. "Come, look what I found."

As he approached, she brushed off the case and held it up to the sunlight peeking through the trees. "Check it out," she said. "My rake hit this when I hauled out that last jumble of vines. I had to dig some to pull it free." She shook the box gently, then, hearing nothing, harder. Something thwacked against the side, and she started.

"Well, go on, open it."

She set the container on the scrubby grass and pulled at the loop on the lid. It didn't move. She examined the seam and tried to loosen the lid with the trowel edge. After a minute of maneuvering the tool back and forth, she was able to prize open the cover. They leaned over the case and stared.

"What is it?" he asked.

"Beats me." She prodded several thick stacks of banded, yellowed papers of varying sizes, some with writing, making sure no uninvited guests had crept in. "Receipts?" She lifted the top bundle and fanned the leaves like a deck of cards. "What the hell . . . money! These are hundreds!" She raised wide eyes toward her husband and saw surprise fill his face. "But what's this other stuff?"

He plucked one of the sheets free and examined it. "It's a bunch of names. And dollar amounts." He looked around their two-acre yard and lowered his voice. "Blackmail lists? Wonder what they did."

She stood and read over his shoulder. "I don't recognize any names. And check out the bills. All of them are old, at least twenty years. What do we do? Keep the money? Rebury it, or just the list? I wonder who those people are."

"And where they are, and if there's any chance they'd come looking for their money. We should bring this inside and do some research." He looked around their property. "Good thing you left some of the bushes for privacy."

They headed to their back porch. She whispered, "And I'm glad you found us a home with a big yard. Even if it was a drug dealer's house. Do you think the box belonged to them?"

"Doubt it." They locked the door behind themselves and set the case on the coffee table. He grabbed his laptop. "The dealers only lived here a couple years. Look where the container was buried, how overgrown all those vines and bushes were. No, you're right. The bills are way older. Besides, if the druggies knew money was here, they'd've spent it."

She nodded. "I admit, every so often I get a creepy feeling, knowing they could be out there, watching us, the house. But we've lived here three years, and no one's made any trouble. Do you think we're in the clear to keep the money?"

"Think so. Read this."

She skimmed the website he'd found. "This says the bills are still legal tender, so we can use them. We'd have to be careful, of course. That's thousands of dollars. Man, this is crazy. But good crazy."

They stared at the money, then at each other. He said, "We can't say a word about this. If anyone ever comes looking, and they know we found the money . . . then what?"

She tapped fingers against her lips and then laughed. "I know how we keep this our little secret. But I can't believe I'm saying this."

He cocked his head, waiting.

"We replant those damn vines."

Primordial Stew

by Mark G. Hammerschick

We're on the cutting edge
sluicing slouching scrunching
hidden in rotted beams
deep rooted
gnarled onion knuckles
scents of veal calves on the hook
glistening gleaming gloaming
we hover
drones on the updrafts
beyond cloud line
above tree line
deep in a memory
of Yellowstone lodgepole pine
where the air is thin
like your moist inner thigh
as you shudder in your dreams
deep in the ambiguity of night
where reality hovers
lightning bugs
zip and zap
zooming
hugging the cross winds
volatile incendiary
isolated embers drift
moments lost
moments gained
and it's those moments

those forgettable slices
glimmers of immortality
that bind us
cosmic dust and glue
emerging from that primordial stew
where everything is possible
and anything goes

Inside the Box

by Ellen P. Holder

G rowing up in a large family, I usually felt overlooked and insig-
nificant. It was easy to escape into daydreams and imagine
a different life for myself. But reality always loomed larger than
my dreams.

I wanted life to be more interesting and exciting. Maybe if I
looked a little closer, I could unravel mysteries, dig up some secrets,
find excitement right under my nose.

Which is why I began wondering about *upstairs*. Or more to the
point, why we didn't have one. We lived in a single-story house. But
from the front walk, I could see a window above the front porch
nestled under the pitched roof. Didn't that indicate a room up
there? Or several rooms?

All these questions ran through my head as I wandered out to
the front yard. Daddy was there tinkering with the lawn mower. I
asked him how we were supposed to get upstairs when there was
no stairway. He told me there was no upstairs. I pointed to the spot
above the porch roof and asked, "Then why is there a window?"

Daddy glanced at the house and wiped his hand on a rag. "That's
just the attic window," he said, then peered into the gas tank.

"Ooh, we have an attic!" I tried to stand still and stop jittering.
"How do you get into the attic without stairs?"

"Through a trap door in the ceiling. It's in the top of your bed-
room closet," he told me. "You use a ladder and then pull yourself
through the opening." He watched me closely, probably not sur-
prised at my questions but wondering what I would do with this
information.

My eyes widened, and ideas rushed into my brain. "What's *in* the attic?" I blurted.

"Ellie, I ain't been in the attic. Just a big, ole, dusty, smelly place. Why don't you go get me some cold water." He wiped sweat from his brow and adjusted his stained cap.

I ran inside and filled a tall glass with ice cubes and tap water. When I carried it to my thirsty father, he took a few gulps, set it on the sidewalk, and reached for his tools.

"Do you reckon the folks that lived here before us left some stuff in that attic?" I stared at the window. "Why don't we go up there and look?"

Daddy sat back on his heels, his forehead wrinkling. "We moved into an empty house, Ellie. They took all their things." His hands were extended in front of him, palms up, in a don't-you-get-it gesture.

I backed off, but my thoughts galloped ahead. He had admitted he'd never been in the attic. How could he be sure it was empty? I didn't dare venture into the attic when Daddy had made it clear he didn't want me up there. Still, I longed to check out it out. I could dream about it. My imagination held lots of possibilities.

Later, I told my younger brother and sister the attic was filled with treasures. They wanted to know what kind of treasures. My voice dropped to an urgent whisper, "Gold and silver coins, pearl necklaces, sparkly diamonds, and rubies." I watched their eyes grow big.

Seeing them fall for my story almost made me believe it myself. They wanted to go into the attic, right then, which I was afraid to do. I told them Mama and Daddy had forbidden us to climb into the attic; it was probably full of snakes and spiders anyway. And I warned them not to mention to anyone what I'd told them. It would be our secret.

Now all three of us were dreaming about the treasure in the attic. Nothing could come of it. Even though anything is possible, I had made it all up, and it couldn't be true. So, I shifted my attention to something else: mama's trinket box.

Our living room had a long shelf along one wall, high up above the doorway. I don't know what its purpose was. It was too high to be a bookshelf and in the wrong place for storage. Eventually,

Mama set some things up there to decorate the shelf: a vase filled with plastic flowers, a handmade basket, a plaster statue of an angel, a world globe—and Mama's box.

It was made of wood with a hinged lid and looked like a treasure chest. I had never seen Mama open the box, but she set it on that shelf, right in the center, like it was the place of honor. The shelf had gathered dust, and Daddy brought in a step ladder so Mama could reach the shelf. While she was dusting, I asked her what was in the chest, as I had asked many times before. She assured me it was empty, just a knickknack for decorating a room.

Wheedling as usual, I asked, "What good is a box if you don't keep anything in it?" I saw the raised eyebrow, my signal to back off before I got her riled up.

"It's just a box," she snapped. "A box doesn't always have to have something inside."

I took my cue and dropped the subject. But I kept eyeing that box and wondering about it. *Was it full of old love letters from Daddy? Was it a secret place to hide money or important papers? Did it hold gifts that Mama treasured or an old photograph I'd never seen?*

Days later, when our parents were back at work, I was left in charge of Mike and Vicky. They helped me drag the ladder back into the living room. This time I would find the answer. Mama would never know I snooped inside her trinket box.

I pulled the ladder close to the wall and climbed up carefully. It wobbled, and I steadied myself. I lifted the box down and raised the lid. My heart raced, and I sucked in a nervous breath.

Inside was a folded paper. I was about to read one of Mama's lifelong secrets. I unfolded the paper and read:

See, there is nothing in the box.
A box doesn't have to have something in it.

I carefully refolded the paper, put it back inside the chest, and left things as I had found them.

_____

Years have passed, and I still look with longing on things that seem unattainable—too high and out of reach. Sometimes, I have the courage to satisfy my curiosity. Sometimes I have the inspiration to pursue my dreams, and some of them have been realized. I've learned that daydreaming isn't all bad. And I've learned that making up stories can be a lot of fun.

As it happens, today I have a small, ornamental box that resembles a treasure chest. It looks good anywhere I place it. I can't decide what to put in the box; it should be exactly the right thing.

I'm sure I'll think of something.

Ramona

by Chris Holmes

"Oh, no. Gwen's back." I shrank away from the narrow opening in the front window drapes.

"Let her in, Alan," Ramona said.

"But she'll see you."

"Let her in. You promised."

Though Ramona's calm monotone never wavered, my hesitation irritated her. The death grip she held on my left wrist tightened, and the spindly thorn embedded in my vein burrowed in deeper.

The doorbell rang followed by a series of loud staccato raps.

I drew in a deep breath, hid my left arm behind my back, and opened the door.

Gwen Shapiro glared up at me. "Mr. Curtis, I'm here about your yard. *Again.*"

A month ago, when we'd first moved into the Blossom Hills subdivision, Gwen had called my wife Debbie and me by our first names. The short, round nosy-body thoroughly enjoyed her role as official HOA greeter. She trolled the neighborhood daily in a golf cart with her frizzy, dyed halo of hair shining like a tangerine in the Florida sun. She used bubbly small talk to glean as much personal information as she could from the residents.

Today, a deep furrow separated her squinty eyes, and her red lips compressed into a tight line.

"I-I'm sorry. My mower broke and I haven't—"

"Had time to get it repaired. That's what you said the last two times. The board's been patient, but the overgrown condition of your yard is appalling. Mow your yard, or call a lawn service. If you don't comply within forty-eight hours, we'll be forced to take harsher actions."

"Please. I need more time."

"Any more time and whatever that purple flowered vine is all over your yard will envelop the entire house. It's a jungle out here. I've never seen anything like it." Gwen's beady eyes narrowed. "You look sickly, Alan. Quite literally, green around the gills. And you're acting strangely. Are you hiding something in there?" Gwen craned her neck to look past me and into the house.

"N-no."

"You know the fines can get pretty steep. Just mow your yard, for heaven's sake."

Ramona's voice hummed in my head. "Invite her in. For Debbie's sake." Gwen showed no indication she'd heard. Until now, I wasn't sure if anyone else could hear Ramona.

"I don't want to," I whispered.

"Are you refusing to comply to HOA rules?" Gwen's eyes widened a bit.

"N-no." A tremor ran through my body when the needle-like thorn jabbed deeper into my wrist. "Come inside so we can . . . talk."

Gwen eyed me for a moment before stepping into the foyer. "Good Lord, it's downright steamy in here. Is your AC broken, too?"

"It's off. Ramona prefers it warm."

"Ramona? Your wife's name is Debbie." Gwen's penciled brows raised. "That explains your odd behavior. Did you two break up?"

A long, leafy vine shot down the hallway. It slammed the door shut behind Gwen.

"What the heck's going on?" Gwen reached for the doorknob. The vine encircled her wrists and pinned both arms to her sides. In a blink, it formed a thick, green belt around her plump waist.

She let out a shocked whimper as the plant tugged her toward the living room.

"It's useless to resist, Gwen." I showed her my left arm. Streaks of green stained my skin from where the thorn had lodged in my vein. The green lines pulsated, spread up my arm, and across my chest. I followed behind as Ramona dragged Gwen into the living room.

Gwen screamed at the sight before her. The walls, floor, and ceiling were covered, and our furniture lay hidden beneath a waist-deep jumble of vines. Droplets of water from the overhead fire sprinkler, which Ramona controlled, dotted the lush leaves. Stunning huge, purple blooms gave off an intoxicating aroma. Ramona really was quite beautiful. I hated to admit it, but I'd come to crave the sweet scent and the euphoric feeling when I breathed it in.

Terrified blue eyes and a nose—the only visible parts of Debbie— peered out beneath a thick mound of leaves and flowers that encased our sofa. The vine twisted tightly across her mouth prevented her from speaking. Ramona used my poor wife as leverage, so I would do her bidding.

"Help!" Gwen screamed and wriggled against the vines in a futile attempt to free her arms. Ramona stifled her cries, rapidly binding her from head to foot until, like Debbie, only her eyes and nose were left exposed.

"Introduce me, Alan," Ramona said.

"G-Gwen, this is Ramona. Debbie found her at the local nursery. You remember she told you she was an avid gardener, right?" My voice broke, and I stared at my wife—her wide eyes glassy with tears. A sharp poke from Ramona brought my focus back to Gwen.

"Deb always checks the discounted plants at the nurseries. They're in poor shape and on a shelf in the back. She says they just need a little extra love and care to flourish. Well, this half-dead seedling she brought home responded to her care astonishingly well. Tripled in size the first day and then kept . . . growing. Within a week it covered all of the flower beds and the lawn. Deb noticed the purple flowers and did some research online. Clematis Standard Ramona. Ow!" The thorn jab scolded me. "I meant Clematis Ramona; she doesn't like to be called standard. She's, uh . . . not at all standard."

I'm not sure if Gwen even heard my babbling. Her stout, vine-wrapped figure trembled, and muffled sobs emanated from within the foliage. My voice barely a whisper, I added, "Ramona didn't like it when Deb tried to trim the vines back. That's when she took control. She had done well on regular fertilizer, but said she needed protein to reach her full potential. She demanded it. I gave her all the meat in the freezer, but it wasn't . . . fresh. I-I'm so sorry, Gwen."

Gwen's vine-cocooned body rose in the air and appeared to float as it passed over a mosh pit of leafy hands. Ramona hefted her out the back door and into the yard.

Not long after, I felt a surge of energy in the vine holding my wrist. The plethora of vibrant purple blooms surrounding me simultaneously emitted bursts of perfumed mist. The heightened scent made me giddy and relieved—Ramona was finally happy.

"Ramona, now that you've had, uh, protein, would you release Debbie? Please."

"Not yet," Ramona replied.

The tears glazing Debbie's eyes spilled over and dribbled onto the leaves under her chin.

"When?" I asked.

The leaves vibrated in tune with a lilting laughter that echoed through the room. "When you bring me more protein, Alan. Lots more."

Beneath Comfort's Shadows

by John Hope

I brace my lower back with one hand as I pick up a steaming pot of coffee with the other. Seven in the morning, and it's already been a long shift for this over-the-hill gal. Meanwhile, the crisp scents of frying butter and bacon hang in the air like a warm, quiet fog.

I shuffle to the far booth where the old man sits reading his newspaper. I top off his mug. "Any news, old man?"

He lowers the newspaper, mumbles something, and taps the opposite side of the table where no one sits. I know he was waiting for his sweet, silvery wife.

The chime of a tiny bell turns me toward the Waffle House entrance. A fat man named Seth and his tubby little boy Bo.

I raise the pot of coffee. "Morning, Seth."

He smiles. "Hey, Lizzy." He takes his normal booth just past the cloudy jukebox that hasn't worked in decades.

I step to the plastic cups near the register, fill up a pair with whole milk, grab a coloring sheet and crayons, and deliver everything to Seth and Bo. "Your usual?"

Seth's round cheeks spread. "Of course."

Bo says, "Extra whip-cweam, pwease."

I ruffle the boy's hair and pass the order to Donny, our short-order cook. I look over my shoulder and, like every Saturday morning, Seth frowns and leans his chin into his hand as Bo scribbles crayons on his paper. Seth smiles every time he walks in, but I know his divorce eats him up inside. Over the past year, I've seen him put on the pounds with every syrup-drowned waffle he scarfs down. He used to be the star quarterback in high school. Now, he barely fits in the booth. And he's dragging Bo with him, making him the poster child for youth obesity. Counseling would do them good. But by the looks of him, he bottles his pain, like most men I've known.

The door chimes. In walk Cleveland and Jack.

"Morning, boys," I greet.

"Hey, Thin Lizzy." Cleveland, the brawny Black man, gives my left butt cheek a quick pat as they step to the end of the counter where they always sit.

We get very few truckers here. This Waffle House was built decades ago when US 41 was the main route between Miami and west Florida. Now, with Alligator Alley in place, truckers have to swing too far out of their way for a couple of oily waffles they could pick up anywhere. But Cleveland and Jack are regulars. They hide their affection for each other from the other manly men in their trucking world and make this dump their surreptitious rendezvous. As big and muscular as they are, they act like a pair of giddy children, as they nudge and giggle together at the counter.

I push their ticket to Donny without asking what they want and deliver a pair of coffees in front of them.

"Thank you, gorgeous." Jack gives me a wink and then refocuses on Cleveland.

Donny dings the bell. I fetch Seth and Bo's plates.

The door chimes. A thin, young lady in a black-and-red business suit steps in. Lips tight, back straight with a leather bag draped over one shoulder. She wasn't the type I was used to seeing.

"Sit anywhere you want," I call to her as I deliver plates.

She nods and finds a booth. From the bag, she pulls out a laptop and opens it.

I arrive with a mug and the coffeepot. "Regular or decaf?"

"W-w-water, please." Her voice shakes like a nervous sparrow.

"Need a menu?"

"Do you have a salad?"

"Not now. We're serving breakfast. It's all grease and butter at the Waffle House."

"Oh. Maybe some toast. No butter."

"You got it."

I return a few minutes later with her order. "Darkened bread on a plate." I place it next to her laptop. "Jelly's on the table."

She grabs the toast and nibbles at the corner.

"Let me know if you need anything."

She nods and returns to her laptop, typing away. We occasionally get people like her: out-of-place and certainly not here for the fine dining experience. She comes for anonymity—a chance to hide away from whatever world she came from and do a little white-collar work. Or maybe to write her great American novel. I never know.

Donny dings the bell, and I serve up more plates. I glance at the scrawny woman and catch her dabbing tears with a napkin. I return to her booth. "You okay, sweetie?"

"Yes. Yes." She hides the dampened napkin. "You know, I think I will have coffee. Caffeinated. Strong."

"You got it." I don't probe. Even with her posh, pin-striped suit and likely success, I sense she's as frail as the rest of us. I keep her pain hidden and tank her up with coffee.

The breakfast crowd comes and goes. Donny keeps the food coming, and the customers keep me moving. Sue starts her shift, and I finally get a reprieve. I take off my apron that reeks of grease and stale coffee and step into the kitchen just behind the wall.

Donny stands over the sizzling grill and reviews the pair of tickets dangling to his left. He angles his head toward me. "Hey, Lizzy." He flips hashbrowns and bacon with the spatula in his three-fingered hand. With his other arm missing, his dirtied, white sleeve is safety pinned near his shoulder. I used to love listening to Donny play piano before a drunk driver took it all away. He'd play the most beautiful pieces in church. Living in the adjacent apartment, I'd hear him rehearsing at night as I sat out on the balcony—cigarette in hand. Now, working in silence, he still amazes me, cooking up the plates, one armed, and ringing his bell. I know how much it pains him to be here rather than in a grand music hall.

I hug him from behind. "You wanna mess around later?"

He smirks. "After you drop off your dad?"

I peck him on the cheek. "See you at home."

I walk to the back booth where the old man still sits. "You ready, Dad?"

He taps the opposite side of the table where no one sits.

"Yes, I know. Mom's not here. She's probably at home right now."

He smiles and nods.

I help him to his feet and walk him to the door. I get waves from the other regulars and, "See you tomorrow, Lizzy!" from a few.

"Mother's at home?" the old man struggles to ask.

"Yeah. Mom's at home." I keep him shuffling forward and shelter Dad's failing mind from the truth—Mom died five years ago. Like everyone else's secrets, I hide his beneath the shadows of warm coffee and Donny's greasy waffles, comforts that help us all get through the day.

The Secret Tourist

by Bart Huitema

Whoever recommended the Key West Express ferry as the best way to see the Florida Keys never rode it through a typhoon. At the halfway point from Fort Myers to Key West, dark clouds enveloped us in a blanket of thunder, lightning, and rain.

Seated in the boat's galley, I gripped my seat as the floor beneath me rolled and swayed. I noticed the guy two seats down from me snoozing away. "Hey buddy." I shook his shoulder. "We just hit a storm that's threatening to swamp the boat. You may want to wake up for this."

The guy yawned and stretched his arms. "We're on a shuttle in the Gulf of Mexico, not an Atlantic voyage. It can't be that bad." He walked toward the window as an enormous wave slammed the side of the ferry sending it rocking. The guy steadied himself against the wall before shuffling toward the exit door.

"I don't think it's wise for you to go out there right now," I told him.

The guy opened the door, stepped outside, and gripped the handrail. He was clearly nuts, but I couldn't let him go out there all by himself, so I followed him.

"Do you have a screw loose?" I shouted over the wind, waves, and rain. "You need to get inside before you get washed overboard."

The guy faced his palm toward the storm and shouted, "Be still."

"I'm just trying to help," I replied.

He turned toward me. "Oh, hey. I wasn't talking to you. I was talking to the storm."

"A lot of good that's going to do you. Come on. Let's get inside."

The guy faced the weather. "No need. We're all good now."

I watched slack-jawed as the dark clouds dissipated, revealing a blue sky; the waves subsided, leaving the Gulf's water calm and clear, and rays of sunshine warmed our drenched clothes.

"I've got to hand it to you," I finally said. "Your timing is impeccable." When he didn't reply, I asked, "What brings you to Florida?"

"I come down here now and then to check up on things."

I extended my hand. "Pleased to meet you. I'm Bart."

He shook it. "My friends call me Jay. I knew a Bartholomew once. Let's head back in."

I glanced down. "Too bad we're soaked to the bone."

He pinched my sleeve. "You look plenty dry to me."

And I was. Totally dry. Not only that, but my clothes smelled just-pressed fresh.

"Why did you pick Key West?" I asked.

"It's a beautiful place."

"I've lived in Florida for twenty years, and I've never seen the Keys, so I thought I'd check it out. Want to hang out, Jay?"

"Sure, Bart. Why not?"

After getting off the boat, we stood at the dock.

"What should we see?" he asked.

I pulled out a brochure. "For starters, there's Mallory Square, the Lighthouse, the Ernest Hemingway House and Museum, and the Aquarium."

"Works for me."

As we waited at an intersection near Mallory Square, a guy on a bike zipped past us. Trusting the walk signal, he failed to check the road for traffic. An SUV sped through the intersection two seconds after the light turned red and slammed into the biker, sending him flying.

"Oh my God," I said. I ran toward the biker; he lie on the street groaning next to his crumpled conveyance. The solid hit broke his leg.

The woman driving the SUV hopped out. "I'm so sorry. I didn't see you. You came out of nowhere."

"Call an ambulance," a bystander shouted.

"No need." Jay offered the biker his hand. "Get up. You're fine."

The biker's look of shock melted when he gazed into Jay's calm blue eyes, and he took the hand.

"Very good." Jay pulled him to his feet.

The biker stood, as if nothing had happened. His leg looked perfectly intact, and his bike looked like new. He brushed himself off. "Thanks, man."

Jay addressed the growing crowd. "Everything's fine." He spoke to the woman driver. "Let's be a little more cautious from now on. Okay, Janet?"

She bowed her head. "Yes, sir."

"And Tony. Look both ways before you cross."

"Yes, sir."

Jay and I continued our walk.

"I know what I saw just now, and I saw what you did to the storm. Who are you?"

"I'm just a humble tourist, like yourself."

"No," I prodded. "Really."

He whispered, "It's a secret."

"Okay."

———

Jay and I checked out the aquarium, Ernest Hemingway's home, and several other attractions. Jay wouldn't talk much about himself. Instead, he quizzed me about my life and what I thought about the state of the world.

On our way to the lighthouse, we passed a marina filled with fishing boats. "I had some wonderful friends who were fishermen," Jay told me.

I motioned toward the boats. "What's odd is that nobody seems to be working."

A voice behind us boomed, "That's because the sea's bone dry. It's been dry for days."

"Maybe you're not fishing in the right spot," I said. "Got your phone?" I turned to Jay. "Everything's computerized nowadays."

"I see."

The guy pulled out his phone, started his navigation app, and handed it to me. I showed the map display to Jay. "Where should he go?"

Jay chuckled before tapping an open section of blue, creating a GPS pushpin. "Try here."

"It's getting late." The fisherman met Jay's eyes. "But I guess I have time for one more run." He hustled back to his boat.

After touring the lighthouse, we stopped at a fish-and-chips place near the marina. The fishing drought had wiped out their fresh seafood selection, so we both ordered the frozen salmon.

Jay took a bite of his meal and grinned. "This tastes very familiar, just like the fish I used to eat in the old days. Red wine would make the meal complete."

"Too bad they only serve beer at this place."

"Such a waste." He glanced around before tapping my water glass. The clear liquid turned red. Tapping his own glass caused a similar result.

I took a bite of my fish and followed it up with a sip of the magical, red liquid. The combination tasted divine. "This is amazing."

He patted my back. "What did I tell you?"

After an incredible meal, we sat on a bench overlooking the marina close to the Key West Express.

"Are you taking the ferry back to Fort Myers?" I asked.

"No. I've seen what I came to see."

"It's been an honor hanging out with you, sir."

"The honor was all mine. It's been a wonderful day." He shook my hand. "Until we meet again, Bart."

"Until we meet again," I replied.

He rose and walked away.

As the sun approached the horizon, the Key West Express pulled out of port. I stood at the railing where Jay had calmed the storm, and I watched the returning ships. A whistle drew my attention to a fishing boat whose bowing deck struggled to support nets overflowing with fish. A familiar fisherman flashed me a thumbs-up sign.

I laughed and flashed one back.

The Toyshop's Secret #10

by Donald Jay

Cheyenne hurried as quickly as her forearm crutches would carry her into the alcove of the doorway to the toyshop. She fished the antique skeleton key from her pocket, turned it in the lock, and bumped the bell with the top of the door as she scooted inside. The bell chimed again as she pushed the door closed. Shedding her coat, she tossed it across the counter next to the life-sized rocking horse tilting back and forth. Leaving the lights off, she made her way to the rotunda and paused in the shaft of moonlight that beamed through the large, round Victorian skylight two stories above.

She gazed up at the three-quarter moon. "Well, I'm here," she muttered, "and I'm late. I know that." The trip from the hospital had chewed up precious time. She paced. "Think, Shy. Think. What exactly did he say before he passed out? 'Protect the . . .' Then some word I couldn't make out. 'The toyshop is the secret.' Then he said 'By midnight. It must be by midnight.'" *Then he collapsed.* Her shoulders dropped.

She scanned the room for a clock. "Are you kidding me? All these mechanical marvels, and Upchurch doesn't even have a clock?" She wiggled her phone from the hip pocket of her tight jeans. *Six minutes to midnight, and I don't even know where to start. Where was Upchurch when he fell? I don't think anyone knows.* She pivoted. The toyshop was as animated at 11:54 at night as at noon. The train click-clacked along the track that extended from the mezzanine level, the biplane's propeller revolved, and toy hot-air balloons floated over the antique Victorian carousel plinking its cheerful tune in the diorama of a county fair.

As far as Shy knew, the toyshop always sounded like this, day or night. *But no, wait, not like this. Something is different.* She looped a strand of her long, jet-black hair over her ear. *The train sounds—* Shy winced when the merry-go-round plunked, drawing her attention. Its giant key stuttered as it turned. Her mouth gaped. The sights and sounds that enchanted the toyshop, that were always there, that never stopped, seemed to be slowing down.

Shy stepped to the dead center of the moon's soft glow. The skylight's frame cast a circle on the floor. The shadow of the train circumnavigating the compass rose beneath her feet, heading south, it chugged almost imperceptibly slower with each puff of smoke from its stack. A zeppelin suspended from the ceiling interrupted the moon's beam at the northern point of the compass, while the shadow of the biplane approached on a collision course from the left. *How can that be?* Shy gazed upward. She had only worked at the toyshop a short time, but she remembered the biplane being hung over there, *or was it over there?* But never so close to the zeppelin, which . . . *wait, wasn't the zeppelin hung closer to the front door?*

She glared upward. The moon's brightness blocked her view of the ceiling around the skylight. She considered returning to the front door to turn on the light, but time was not on her side. Instead, she scrambled up the winding staircase at the center of the store to the mezzanine level, a feat made challenging by her crutches, and peered over the railing. Then, looking up, she illuminated the ceiling with her phone's flashlight app. The biplane and the zeppelin were suspended from rods protruding from tracks in the ceiling. She had never noticed it before, but they moved. She peered over the railing again at the shadows below.

That's what Upchurch was trying to tell me. He doesn't have a clock because he doesn't need a clock. The toyshop is a clock! The toyshop is the secret. Dread washed over her. She checked her phone. *Three minutes to midnight. The biplane is approaching the zeppelin at twelve o'clock, and the train isn't going to make it around three more times. The toyshop is winding down.*

Recalling the desperate look in Upchurch's eyes made her shudder. Shy didn't know what the toyshop protected, but preventing it from stopping meant everything to that old toymaker. She had to make it happen.

Opening her palms, she scanned the mezzanine level and the main floor below. "How do I wind a whole toyshop?" She pushed her hair from her forehead. "How do you wind a clock?" She raised one eyebrow. "I need a key." Scanning the store again with her cellphone's flashlight, she paused on the beam at the country fair diorama. Her jaw dropped, and her eyes locked on the giant key of the carousel. "Ask and ye shall receive."

She almost tumbled down the winding staircase and raced over to the diorama. The large tin key clicked and faltered. She ditched her crutches and turned the key with both hands. It turned easily at first and stiffened the more she turned. She paused. The carousel slowed to a stop. The train fell silent. The biplane's propeller froze. The rocking horse stopped. The toyshop grew still. She checked the time: 11:59.

"Oh, no. No, no, no, no, no. You can't stop. I'm so close!" she shouted. Racking her brain for anything else she might do, she remembered watching her Uncle Charley wind the grandfather clock in the general store. She saw him in her mind's eye, pulling up the counterweights of the old clock. She scanned the diorama for anything that resembled counterweights. The hot-air balloons had landed and were sitting on the fake grass. She followed the two loops of chain they rode on to the rear of the Ferris wheel. Cautiously turning the carnival ride by hand sent the two hot-air balloons up to their clouds. She released the Ferris wheel and paused. Nothing.

Time had to be almost up. "What am I missing?" she asked aloud. She pounded her temples. *You wind the clock, you pull up the weights, and you start the pendulum. The pendulum. That's it. I need a pendulum.* She hustled to the center of the shop. *What in this toyshop could be a pendulum?* "Grant said Upchurch fell. He fell . . . down, that wouldn't give him a concussion. He fell from a ladder? He fell down the stairs?" She threw up her arms. "Who knows? Maybe he was thrown from a horse." She pivoted toward the front door. *A horse! A rocking horse.* She charged across the store to the huge rocking horse near the door. She tugged on the handle, trying to get it to rock. It wouldn't move. Dropping her crutches and summoning every ounce of strength she could muster, she swung herself onto the saddle and flung her body forward and backward until the horse rocked.

The train wheels clacked, the biplane propeller rotated, and the carousel filled the store with its sweet melody. The toyshop was alive once more.

Shy dismounted and peeked at her cell phone. *Midnight.* "You know," she said to the horse, now rocking on its own, "when that old man wakes up, he's got some explaining to do."

Truck Stop

by Beda Kantarjian

Allison's fearless enthusiasm swept me up in her plans before I could remember who I was: a cautious housewife and mother whose husband would be suspicious about a job we'd plucked out of the classifieds—if I'd told him. That's how we ended up at a truck stop parking lot waiting for our new employer. There had been no interview, no exchange of the usual employment information. We would simply do a job and be paid when completed, according to the ad. And we'd be home before my kids got out of school.

We parked at the far corner of the lot, where instructed, and waited. Nearby, several cars gathered with one or more women looking as skeptical as me. Not Allison. She sat sipping her coffee in the same casual manner she had when we fought issues affecting our neighborhood at county commission meetings.

Allison carried her extra weight, plain face, and blunt-cut hair with nonchalance; whereas I, with a thirtieth birthday looming, exercised daily, kept my roots blond, and never stepped out the door without full makeup. Yet, somehow, we made a powerful team.

Five minutes after the appointed time, I spotted a white-paneled van parked near the fueling pumps moving toward us. It came to a stop, and a muscular woman with blond, over-dyed hair hopped out and swept an arm in our direction to summon us.

"What have we got to lose?" Allison said with a playful smile.

I could think of a few things. What if this "company" isn't what we're told it is? What if this is a ruse to get us here and traffic us at the truck stop and beyond? Why in the world did I go along with my friend's crazy scheme? But how else would I save enough to buy my husband that fish finder for Christmas? It would all be worth it when I saw his face Christmas morning.

"Are you coming?" Allison had already hopped out of the car.

I grimaced and slowly exited her vehicle. We joined the other young women, about five or so, slowly walking toward the woman with an arm full of papers.

"Sorry I'm late, but nice to see a good crowd. Your job is to go door to door until we cover the whole Palmetto subdivision. At each home, you'll give the owner a flyer with our special bicentennial rates and schedules. They sign on the spot, you earn a bonus, and they get a better rate by signing up before the end of '76. As you know, South Carolina garbage service runs on independent companies. We have better equipment and more of it than the company currently picking up garbage in the Palmetto subdivision. Ready, ladies?"

So far, things were going as advertised. As usual, I'd worried for nothing.

The rusty backdoor hinges squawked as she opened them. She motioned for us to get in.

"What did you get us into, Allison?" I whispered.

"Come on. This is how we do things in South Carolina. You're not in Virginia anymore."

As the women hoisted themselves into the van, slowly at first, laughing nervously, a picture flashed into my head. *La Dolce Vita*. In previews for that old movie starring Shirley MacLaine, she and other prostitutes piled into a van. A police van, but still . . . I grabbed Allison's shirt and pulled her back. She shook me off and climbed in, then offered me her hand. We settled at the back end of a side bench.

The door banged shut, and keys rattled. Allison cut her eyes at me and lurched toward the door. She pushed the handle slightly down and held on tightly. We heard the fumbling of keys, a "Damn!" and then keys hitting the pavement. Allison's eyes were as wide as mine felt as we leaned toward the door, listening for another attempt, but instead the engine started, and we lurched forward.

"Are we being stupid?" I asked. "Maybe she wanted to protect us with a locked door. If she weren't legit, would she have all those printed flyers?"

Allison and I moved back onto the bench. Only a small, flickering roof light illuminated the windowless van, heightening my senses. What I wouldn't give for Chuck's CB radio now, just in case. We all sat quietly, lost in our thoughts, until our bodies leaned into the pressure of a turn.

A quick squeeze on my arm told me Allison also realized we hadn't turned left toward Palmetto. She dropped to her knees and told me to follow, then crawled to the back door. I made out her hand on the door handle as she motioned for me to crouch and brace myself like she had. We could smell diesel fumes from trucks ahead of us and feel the slow pull of the van on an incline. The ramp to the interstate!

Time stood still until Allison pulled down hard on the door handle. Gravity flung the doors open, and Allison's unnecessary kick propelled her body to the pavement. I exhaled with a prayer, jumped out, then rolled down the side of the embankment following Allison's lead. Two ladies came tumbling after us. We all quickly checked for serious injuries and, though we'd been bruised and scraped, our bones seemed fine. The slow pace of the trucks in front of us had been in our favor.

"Y'all okay?"

The other ladies nodded. We all looked toward the van, still climbing the interstate ramp. Apparently, our captor, focused intently on whatever she had in mind, hadn't noticed.

"Do y'all know any of the ladies still in the van?" I asked.

"No, we came alone. Maybe they didn't pick up on what y'all were doing the way we did."

The run back to the parking lot left us panting. Only when safely locked in Allison's car did we relax. Allison turned the key, and her car radio blasted ABBA's "Dancing Queen." She switched to the local news.

"Oh my God, this will be on the news if it's as bad as we think." I buried my head in my hands. "What will I tell Chuck?"

Allison jumped out and ran to the car near us with the two ladies, said a few words, and ran back.

"What did you say to them?"

"I told them to run into the truck stop and call South Carolina Highway Patrol. They will rescue the other ladies, and we'll be long gone by the time they get here. Don't worry, Chuck will never know the mess I got you into." Allison pressed her lips in a forced smile and patted my hand. "I don't want to lose my adventure buddy."

After dinner Chuck and I settled on the porch with a glass of wine.

"So, how did your day go?" Chuck asked.

Across the street Allison stepped onto her porch and waved.

I shrugged. "Same old, same old."

Fallen Apples

by Henry James Kaye

Harold glanced at the clock above the bar. "Damnit! I should have left fifteen minutes ago." Tiffany's cleavage had made him late, again. Now he'd disappoint his wife and son, again.

He dropped forty dollars on the bar, waved at Tiffany, rushed out, and quick-marched to the subway entrance. At the bottom of the stairs—short of breath and hurrying around a blind corner—he collided with a vendor table, fell to the cold concrete floor, and slid several feet.

Scrambling upright, Harold shoved through the turnstile and arrived on the platform in time to see his train disappear into the black tunnel. He raised a middle finger and shouted, "You son-of-a-bitch, you left early."

His thigh hurt. His wrist stung. He looked down and discovered a hole in his pants and blood on his hand. Harold decided to give that damn vendor a piece of his mind for setting the frickin' table too close to the walkway. He pushed through the exit roundabout and stormed back to the vendor area.

The table still lay on its side. A shabbily dressed girl, about twelve years old, on her hands and knees, slowly moved her hand in an arc about an inch off the concrete. She stopped when her fingers encountered a green apple. The young girl wrapped her fingers around it, felt its surface, then held it to her nose. She frowned and put the apple in a jacket pocket, crawled forward a couple of feet, and repeated the sweeping movements again.

Harold approached, ready to yell at her for setting the table around a blind corner and being a tripping hazard.

She lifted her head. White orbs, no pupils, sat where eyes should have been.

Harold's breath caught, and his heart skipped a beat.

"Please mister, don't step on my apples."

"Huh?" Then he noticed an apple at his feet, picked it up, and extended his arm. "This apple's yours?"

The girl reached out.

Harold moved the apple until it touched her hand. She wrapped her fingers around it, sat back on her feet, felt it with fingertips, and sniffed it. She smiled and clutched it to her chest like it was the dearest thing in the world to her. "Thanks, mister. I'm still missing five. Do you have time to help me find them?" The girl struggled to her feet—head tilted as if listening for an answer.

Harold forgot about his pains. "Sure." He retrieved three nearby apples and handed them over, one by one.

The girl repeated the process of feeling, sniffing, and putting them in jacket pockets, which now bulged.

"Thank you, sir. One of them is still good. I'll have to pay Mr. Mendelstein for the other two. Are there any more?"

"Let me look around." Harold's stomach sank. Had he really said "look" to a blind girl? He changed the subject. "Who's Mr. Mendelstein?"

"He owns the produce store below our apartment. I buy apples from him, sneak down here, and sell them while my mother's at work." She raised a finger to her lips and smiled. "It's a secret; Mommy doesn't know. Whatever I don't sell, Mr. Mendelstein takes back as long as they're in good shape."

"How do you know they're good?"

"First, I feel them. If there's little indentations, they've been bruised. Then I sniff them. If I can smell the juice, I know they've been bruised. Most of the apples knocked off my table are bruised. I'll have to take money out of my surprise-sack to buy tomorrow's apples."

"Surprise-sack?"

The girl smiled. "That's where I keep the money I make. I want to buy Mommy a bottle of real pretty perfume from the drugstore for her birthday next week."

Harold's heart felt a tug. "That's sweet."

"Mommy sells candy at the next station down the line. She says a lot of people don't notice her table. So, I bet if she had real pretty perfume, riders will notice her and buy candy."

A tear formed in Harold's eye as he wondered if his twelve-year-old son would sell apples in the subway to buy him a present. "That's really thoughtful of you."

"I know it's not easy taking care of a blind kid. There's lots of extra expenses, and I can't help like I want, but I bet giving her the perfume will help make things better."

"How much more do you need for the perfume?"

"Before tonight I still needed nineteen dollars. With the bruised apples I have to pay for," her voice cracked, "I'm not sure how I'll get it done, but I'll keep praying. Mommy says when you want something really bad to pray to God, and he'll come help."

"Your mother must be very proud of you."

"She tells me all the time." She smiled and nodded, then her forehead wrinkled. "I'm sorry sir, but do you know where my last two apples are? Maybe they're okay, and I won't have to take as much out of my surprise-sack." She tilted her head.

Harold looked around. "They rolled through the turnstile."

"Thank you. I'll ask someone going through if they'd hand them to me so I don't have to pay."

Harold smiled for the first time that day. "I'll get them" He pulled out his transit card, slid it through the reader, and side-stepped through the turnstile. After retrieving the apples, he exited through the barred roundabout and handed them over.

The girl felt, then sniffed each. Her shoulders sank, and the smile disappeared. "Both are bruised, but thank you for your time. Not many people would help a blind kid in the subway. They're in too much of a hurry, like the guy that knocked over my table. I hope you have a good evening."

Harold stiffened. "I'm the asshole that knocked over your table."

The girl's hand flew to her mouth. "Oh, I'm sorry. I'm sure it was an accident, and you've helped me a whole lot." She nodded.

"That's okay. My priorities have been mixed up this evening." Harold took a twenty-dollar bill from his wallet, paused, slid it back in, then extracted a fifty. "You and your mother deserve better than what life's given you." He took her hand and put the bill in it. "Here's fifty dollars. Now you can buy the perfume and stay home, safe from assholes like me."

She pulled her hands into her chest, clutching the bill. "I...I...I don't know what to say."

"No need to say anything. You've taught me an important lesson about my own apples."

"Your apples?" Her forehead wrinkled again.

He wagged his head and smiled. "Never mind, I'm being silly."

"Sir, can I ask you a question?"

"Sure."

"Did God send you?"

Harold stiffened, and his stomach knotted. He patted her shoulder. "No, but I think he sent you to me. I have to get home. Goodbye and good luck." He side-stepped through the turnstile again as another train rumbled into the station. Harold paused and watched her tuck the bill into a pocket. He then considered the apples in his own life that had become bruised. He rubbed his scraped hands together and vowed to find a large bottle of perfume.

The Little Tin Box

by Tami Kidd

My sister took possession of the box after my mother passed away. I was thirty years old at the time, but I was twelve when the little tin box changed my life.

My mother's voice called to me that morning, "Tami, I'm going fishing before it gets too hot out." Living in central Arkansas gave her access to many lakes; her favorite was a short distance from our home.

Mom had to walk through my room to get to her bedroom and our lone bathroom. I tried to ignore her, but every time she passed through, the floor squeaked with her heavy footfalls.

Pulling my pillow over my head, I hoped sleep would return. It was Saturday, and sleeping late was my reward for dragging my happy butt to school every day at the crack of dawn.

"Did you hear me?" Mother walked through my room again.

I threw my pillow at the bathroom door after she closed it. "Yes! I heard you."

When she exited, she tossed the pillow back on my bed. "I'll probably be back before it heats up too much. Do you want to go?"

I covered my eyes with my arms. "No! Bye." She knew I hated fishing.

The front door closed, and the car tires munched the gravel in our driveway. I stayed in bed for a while, but sleep didn't come.

I made my way to the kitchen for cereal. As I savored the sweet, fruity nuggets of wholesome goodness, the cereal box captured my attention for a long time. But after that, there was nothing left to occupy me.

It was 1971. Music came via radio, eight-track, or cassettes. Television came through one of the three channels, four if you counted PBS. I tuned my little transistor radio to a local FM station. It played all the greatest hits of the time. Rock was my music of choice, because I was cool.

Dancing to Three Dog Night, I made my bed. It passed my inspection, but my mother would find something about it to criticize. She was like that. If I swept the floor, she was quick to say, "You missed a spot." Or when I washed dishes, "You need to wash the glasses first and pans last," or "These towels aren't folded right." At times I felt like an underappreciated, underpaid maid.

I was bored. So, I did what most kids would do at that age—I snooped. Curiosity flowed through my veins like the minnows in the creek next to our house. On more than one occasion, my mother called me nosey. *Interested* is the word I would use.

My snooping began in my mother's bedroom. It was a large room with a full-size bed and a twin bed. Sometimes, on stormy nights, Mom would insist I sleep in the twin bed. She was terrified of storms, and I think having me in the room gave her comfort. I remember her warnings: "Tami Lynn, get away from that window; you'll get struck by lightning," or "You can't take a bath until this storm passes." My favorite was: "Don't pet that dog; they attract lightning."

To this day, I have not developed a fear of thunderstorms that could compare to hers. Growing up in Tornado Alley gave me a healthy respect. However, they never made me shake and shudder like they did my mother.

———

My dad passed away six years earlier, not long after we moved from California. My sister married and left home the same year. It was getting harder and harder to picture my dad in my mind. Sadness still overcame me when he entered our conversations, which wasn't often, as my mother didn't like bringing up his name.

The photos in the little tin box helped keep his memory alive. It had been around all my life. Longer than he had.

About the size of a woman's shoe box, the brown paint had chipped, and rust peeked through the metal surface. It had a little silver handle and lock but was never locked. Maybe my mother should have locked it.

On my hands and knees, I reached for the box where it resided with a family of dust bunnies under her bed. Sitting on the hardwood floor with my back against the bed, I opened the lid.

My mother often dragged the box out to share her pictures from years long past. She knew most of the people in the black-and-white photos. I didn't pay much attention to the names. The pictures were my focus.

The subjects, with their pinched, serious faces, slicked-backed hair, and drab outfits, made me wonder about their lives. Were they nice people? What were their lives like? Why didn't they smile? In one photo, my father stood in an orange grove. The ground beneath him was dry and cracked—even his dark work boots were chalky-white with dust. The leaves on the orange trees drooped like a sad clown's smile. Southern California must have had a drought that year. I stared at his face and tried to imagine what he was thinking at that moment. He didn't smile either.

The tin box possessed a cache of pictures, letters from my uncles; telegrams from the War Department informing my grandmother her one son suffered injuries, and the other reported missing in action during WWII. I found twenty-year-old receipts for furniture long replaced. Opening the box was like time traveling. I loved it. Until that day.

By the time I made my way to the bottom of the box, it seemed like I had been sitting on the floor for hours. Ready to return the contents and close the lid, something at the bottom caught my eye: a pretty, linen cloth with cute, little flowers embroidered on it. It was yellow with age but stiff with starch. Something was wrapped inside. I unfolded the cloth with slow, delicate movements—like it was a precious gift. Excited curiosity coursed through my veins. It was no gift.

I unfolded the papers hidden in the cloth. I read them. Again, I read them confused by the language. What did Change of Name Adoption mean?

Time stood still, until I grasped what I had in my hands. In a blink, the world changed forever. My parents kept the secret that I was not their child. I belonged to someone else. My name wasn't even mine. I had been named Peggy Jean. Did I have brothers and sisters? Did I look like my mom or my dad? My mind exploded with questions. The emotions I felt couldn't be identified. They never existed before that day.

Tears flowed, and my hands shook as I replaced the papers. A second set of papers were my sister's adoption records. Did she know she was adopted? Did she know I was adopted?

The little tin box turned out to be the keeper of secrets. I felt like the people in the old photos with their somber expressions frozen for all time. I, also, might never smile again.

An Old, Cold Secret

by Michele Verbitski Knudsen

Madeline, my dear friend and neighbor, lay dying in the next room. Her secret would be exposed the minute she took her last breath. Had the statute of limitations run out for the part I played? At eighty-five, acting forgetful seemed to be my best option.

I left Father Conley in the bedroom. Madeline insisted the young priest administer last rites and hear her somewhat befuddled confession. *Even a lapsed Catholic can try to balance the books before she meets her maker.*

I stood at her kitchen window, mesmerized by the silent, flashing lights of the ambulance reflected in our courtyard fountain. Shimmering sprays shot into the air like fireworks: a dazzling display to celebrate Madeline's life.

The EMTs returned to their ambulance and waited. Madeline had refused to go with them. She wanted to die in the home she loved.

Father Conley staggered into the kitchen, his eyes vacant. He hugged a thick padded envelope to his chest.

"Please, Father, have a seat. Let me pour you a brandy."

He plopped down, dropping the envelope on the table.

I poured us each a snifter. "Here, Father."

He took the glass, stared at it, then took a long swig and coughed. "She's . . . with God now."

I swallowed, relishing the warmth as the brandy flowed down my throat. "Your first . . . death on your own?"

He took another swallow, closed his eyes, and nodded.

"Madeline explained?"

His eyes focused, and he turned toward me. "Sort of." He cringed. "She made me promise to pray . . . in the pantry."

I tried to hide my smile. Madeline told me she wanted Fred to have the prayers he never got years ago when he died suddenly of a heart attack.

"Father, the letter for the lawyer—don't you need to call him now?"

His brow furrowed as he examined it. "Reads 'upon my death,' so I better."

"He'll know what to do."

"Very . . . unusual circumstances." His hands shook slightly as he took out his phone.

I left to give him some privacy and peeked in the bedroom. Madeline's lavender fragrance lingered. I took in a deep breath, confident that I did the right thing for her.

Madeline's eyes were open, so I closed them, her skin already cool. I understood the priest's reluctance to touch the body. Many people felt that way. I hoped he didn't freak out saying a prayer for dear, old Fred when I opened the pantry.

Father Conley lightly knocked on the open door. "Attorney's on his way. Not sure I explained things well, but I believe he got the gist of it."

"Good. Another brandy?" I eyed the empty glass in his hand.

"I . . . better not."

"I'll make coffee."

He followed me to the kitchen and sat while I put a pot on to brew.

I didn't want to force him, but if he was going to say a prayer for Fred, he'd better do it now, before all hell broke loose in here.

"Father, why not say Fred's prayer before the lawyer arrives."

He stared at me, grimaced, and swallowed.

I opened the pantry doors and exposed a large chest freezer. "Fred's in there, but I don't think you have to actually see him for the prayer. I'll go next door to my apartment and get the cookies I baked."

I left him standing in front of the freezer.

I warmed and packed the oatmeal raisin cookies. As I started across the courtyard, a Lexus pulled in front. I waved to the tall man getting out of his car. "I'm Sandy Warren, Madeline's neighbor. You must be her attorney."

"Yes. Sam Goodwin." He pressed his lips in a thin smile and shook my hand.

"Come this way. Father Conley's waiting."

We entered to find the priest kneeling on the kitchen floor in front of the freezer. He grabbed the edge of the chest to stand on unsteady legs. He extended his hand. "I'm Father Conley. You must be Mr. Goodwin."

"Yes. What's this all about?"

The priest handed him the envelope. "Hopefully, this explains everything."

Goodwin sat at the kitchen table, and Father Conley joined him. I poured coffee and set a plate of warm cookies between them. The aroma of sugar, cinnamon, and freshly brewed coffee seemed to relax both men. No one uttered a word as the attorney read through the papers.

Goodwin heaved a sigh and chuckled. "Well, I'll be damned." He snagged a few cookies and drank the rest of his coffee. "Let's get this show on the road, shall we?"

He called 911. After a few brief sentences, he ended the call. "Better clear this away. Wouldn't want the police to think we delayed calling just to enjoy your delicious cookies. Besides, in a few minutes, people will be swarming all over this kitchen."

I washed the mugs, wiped the table, and wrapped up the cookies as the sirens grew louder.

"Mr. Goodwin, should Father and I go to my condo?"

"Good idea. They'll want to talk to you both, so stick around, but I'll be present."

Father and I nodded and left. As I closed my condo door, a police cruiser pulled up.

We sat in my kitchen. Police cars and a coroner's van clogged the road. Men and women streamed through the courtyard.

"Father, let's go to the living room."

He sat on the sofa, and I settled in my overstuffed chair placing my aching feet on the matching burgundy ottoman.

Fred and Madeline married late in life. When Fred realized Madeline would never be able to afford their condo once he died, he bought the freezer and enlisted my help when the time came.

Madeline needed both their Social Security checks plus his pension, which ended upon his death, in order to stay.

"Madeline loved this place," I said. "The palm trees, the fountains, and flowering bougainvillea and hibiscus. Until last month, when she broke her hip, she played bingo every Friday and poker every Tuesday afternoon. She said Fred planned all this . . . for her."

A knock on the door brought the priest to his feet. "I'll go." Father brought in the lawyer and a uniformed policeman.

The officer scribbled on a notepad. "Mrs. Warren, when did you find out about the body in the freezer?"

"This morning, right before Madeline passed away. At first, I didn't believe her."

"Quite shocking." Father Conley wrung his hands.

The officer turned toward me. "Think it's been about five years since her husband's been gone?"

"Could be. At my age, years fly by. Thought he left her . . . husbands do."

"Anything else, officer?" the lawyer asked.

"Nope. If both deaths are natural, we'll be good to go."

I walked them to the door. Father Conley and the officer went out.

Mr. Goodwin stayed behind. "I'll sell the condo, make reparations to Social Security and Fred's pension fund, and call you for the reading of the will."

"Thank you." Did that twinkle in his eyes mean Goodwin knew?

After he left, I poured myself a large brandy and settled in my chair. I raised my glass. "Here's to you, Freddy. I took good care of Madeline till her dying day, and she never found out about us, my love."

The Road to Hell

by Linda Kraus

My mother fiercely believed
the road to Hell was paved
with good intentions.
She stitched that abomination
in a florid, floral needlepoint
hung in an old-fashioned frame
above our kitchen sink.

As a child, I loathed
her mantra although
it certainly applied to me.
I squirmed and lied
and insisted it was she
who didn't understand.
My actions were noble;
I had never disobeyed.

When I grew older,
I uttered her trite homily
to my sons: a painful,
demeaning epiphany.
They ignored my words
and looked to the heavens,
proffering absurd proofs
of their innocence.

The secret was out:

without my noticing,
inexplicably, I had
become my mother.
She would have been
surprised that she was
finally vindicated:
her dictum, so long
repressed, rose up,
like a mummy's hand,
and silenced me.

Narrow #4

by Andrea W. LeDew

Down where the river is narrow,
Down where cicadas still sing,
Down where the river is narrow,
Down will I fall on my knees.

Down where the crosses are burning,
Down where they punch their fists high,
Down where the river is narrow,
Down will I lay me to die.

Down where the river is narrow,
Down where the North meets the South—
South, and the river gets wider,
North, and it gapes at the mouth—

Down where I raised all my children,
Down where palmetto leaves spike,
Down where the lizards roam freely,
Down, where we do what we like,

Down where we fight and we argue,
Down where the bravest of men
Court the most beautiful women,
Toast, that the South rise again,

Down where the oak trees are aged,
Branches remembering when

Rope used to drape from the highest,
Taut with the bodies of men,

There, we forget all our troubles,
Centuries, ground in the sand,
Memories, misty, forgotten—
Nothing you would understand.

Even our children know nothing,
History shamed from the shelves.
Down where the river is narrow,
We keep our guilt to ourselves.

The Drawing

by Joan Levy

Fall, 1970

I don't remember why I stole the doll.
However, I vividly recall my teacher's private conversation with me about a doll missing from the dollhouse in our first-grade classroom. Mrs. Reynolds called me to her desk one afternoon after the doll's disappearance.

I walked slowly past peers who drew colorful shapes on construction paper. They stopped their busywork as I moved past each of them. A whisper from one pesky boy to another elicited giggles from both. A communal ear turned toward the front of the room when I approached Mrs. Reynolds. "Children, please continue with your work," she said.

Mrs. Reynolds swiveled her desk chair to face me. She smiled and leaned forward with open hands. She sandwiched my hands between her warm fleshy palms. We faced each other in profile to the students.

Her plump face moved nearer mine, until it filled all but the periphery of my view. She smelled like Pond's Cold Cream. My grandma used Pond's. Chalky-white face powder coated her face, making facial hairs stand erect between her upper lip and nostrils. I stared at her red lips as they mouthed words that hung in the space between her mouth and my ears. I finally heard my name.

"Joanie. Joanie, did you borrow something from the dollhouse?" she queried in a gentle low tone.

"No, ma'am," I answered.

"It seems our mother doll disappeared from the dollhouse."

I stood motionless, unsure whether I needed permission to breathe.

"Would you happen to know where she is?"

"No, ma'am."

Mrs. Reynolds shifted her position in the chair. "Is there anything you'd like to tell me about the doll?"

"No, ma'am."

"We all miss her. Perhaps she'll turn up soon."

Mrs. Reynolds paused, tilted her chin downward, and stared into my eyes. She gave my hands a quick squeeze and released them.

"You may take your seat now."

"Yes, ma'am." My knees wobbled when I turned away from her.

I'd never surrender the mother doll. She belonged to me, and I needed her.

Maybe someone witnessed my brazen act. Someone snitched—probably those pesky boys. They snickered when I walked back to my desk.

"Boys, please step forward to show the class your artwork," said Mrs. Reynolds. "Whew," I said under my breath and felt relief from her distraction.

The three-by-two-foot dollhouse sat on a shelf beneath a bank of large-paned windows and to the left of twenty-seven neatly arranged student desks. My desk sat in a row nearest the dollhouse. Bright sunlight flickered between branches of century-old oak trees outside. The movement cast showy patterns on the house and its contents. The dollhouse family included a father, two children, a dog, and the mother—that is, until I pilfered the mother doll.

When I neared my desk behind Patty Randall's desk, she shoved her artwork in my face. Patty pointed to a stick figure with blond pigtails. "That's you," she said, "and that's the—"

I smacked the drawing with both hands. I hated that girl! I'd hate her forever.

My mother's *do-right* words rushed to mind: "Ignore it, smile, or say thank you." My father's *do-right* words contrasted with my mother's: "Beat their ass," he'd say.

I scooted into my seat. My father's response overrode my mother's kind words. I leaned forward. "You stink. And your ugly freckles stink," I whispered, before I grabbed Patty's copper-colored pony-tail. I yanked it hard.

"Ouch!" she yelped.

"Girls," Mrs. Reynolds said, "please turn your attention to the boys' presentation, or bring your conversation to my desk."

Throughout our school years, I disliked Patty Randall, though I forgot why.

Class of 1982, Ten-Year Reunion

Crepe-paper streamers in purple and black class colors hung draped over welcome banners that decorated the ballroom's double-door entrance. When we entered, my husband and I gazed around the room abuzz with hobnobbing classmates and others.

"I wonder if I'll recognize the adult versions of those kids," I said.

As if on cue, two women encircled me with hugs. "Joanie, you haven't changed in all these years," they squealed and dashed off.

"Not a clue," I said before my husband asked if I recognized them.

A woman, with copper-colored hair styled in a chic up-do, reached for my hands.

"Here's another guess-who," my husband whispered.

Her vibrant hair color and freckled face sparked a vague memory, but I resorted to a glance at her nametag: Patricia (Randall) Moffitt.

"Um . . . Patricia? I don't . . ."

"Everyone knew me as Patty."

Her freckles and hair color stirred my memories, until her name registered. "First grade Patty?" I asked. "For reasons I don't recall, I pulled your ponytail."

"That's me. And my scalp hurt for days," she said.

We embraced and giggled like teenagers over our long-ago antics. My husband slipped away for a beverage, while Patty and I chitchatted.

"Hey, is it too late to ask forgiveness for causing your pain?" I asked in jest.

"Maybe I should ask *your* forgiveness," Patty said.

Her request caught me off guard. "Whatever for?" I asked.

"One afternoon, while Mrs. Reynolds spoke with you at her desk, I drew a special picture for you. I hoped you'd love it. Instead, you pulled my ponytail."

"But why did I pull your hair?" I asked.

"Well . . . because my picture revealed . . . your secret."

"*My* secret?"

"I saw you tuck the dollhouse mother doll into your pants pocket on the previous day. I told Mrs. Reynolds. She said your mother 'had gone to heaven' the summer before we started first grade, and you missed her. She said she'd speak to you. She asked me to keep your deed a secret, which I obeyed—except for the drawing."

"I now remember your artwork," I said. "A girl with yellow pigtails, and in her hand, she held . . . the dollhouse mother doll. The drawing proved you knew about my theft, and you snitched."

"Yes, but there's more to the story," said Patty. "I meant the drawing as a friendship pact between us. But the plan backfired."

"And . . . I pulled your hair, and I disliked you for no reason," I said.

"So it seems."

Patty's tears and mine flowed into a boo-hoo mess. We hugged and forgave each other our childhood misunderstandings.

"By the way, what happened to the drawing after the classroom drama?" I asked.

Patty shrugged. "My mother saved *all* my artwork and that one in particular."

"Ah, the evidence."

"And what happened to the mother doll?" Patty asked.

"She sits on my nightstand as a reminder of my mother. I named her Bunny."

"Bunny?" Patty asked. "Why?" She snickered.

"You know . . . because of her bun hairstyle," I said.

Patty's tickle prompted our belly-laughs until we leaned on each other for support.

My husband returned with a glass of wine for each of us. "Looks like you two rekindled an old relationship," he said.

"I propose a toast," I said and lifted my glass. "Here's to Bunny, to the drawing, and to the surprising reunion between two *new* friends."

Thistle and Weeds

by Kimberly Lewis

In spring, secrets grow on the side of the road.
Wild azalea and swamp iris
dress them up in pink and purple.

In summer, secrets make the grass greener.
They pour from the sky, night after night,
in heavy plops of falling whispers.

In fall, they turn the leaves to new colors,
as autumn wind spreads its blush
throughout the forest.

In winter, secrets warm by a fire,
filling hearths and hearts
the way a quilt gives comfort.

I daresay the secrets of a season
are not only about its beauty.
They also offer wisdom.

So maybe the pretty ones are not the only flowers
with secrets to share in spring.
Thistle in the weeds may hold some secrets, too.

But how much easier it is to pick
soft green stems
than thorny prickle.

To select the flower
that perfumes the air
and looks the best on the kitchen table.

Then blooms the question,
if we avoid the thistle,
do we overlook something important?

Because look how a butterfly hovers so near,
though thistle could tear its fragile wing.
Or is this a secret the butterfly reveals?

To our eye, it lights in a place that's unexpected,
as if nature tries to tell us that what we seek
is not always where we would think.

That we may have to wander into some thorns
in order to fill our deepest wants.
Sometimes to find the most precious gifts,

we may need to look in thistle and weeds.

A Well-Kept Martian Secret

by Lawrence Martin

September 2037

T hree months out from Earth, the Orion-3 Spaceship entered low Mars orbit. Voice communication with NASA had ceased a month out as the transmission delays made speaking to Mission Control Center tedious. Now in orbit around Mars, the delay was thirteen minutes each way.

For the four-man Orion crew, NASA's excitement and encouragement in text messages were most welcomed. After two failed attempts to reach Mars, Orion-3 was going to succeed. The first attempt, in 2033, used liquid fuel propulsion, which mandated an eight-month voyage. Skeptics warned NASA this was too long, but volunteers were aplenty, and a six-person crew took off from Earth with great anticipation. It was not the journey's length that doomed the voyage; two months out, radiation sickness took its toll with two severely ill astronauts, and the ship was ordered back home.

The second attempt, in 2035, incorporated a thicker hull and a switch to nuclear propulsion, but there were glitches. What was planned as a five-month journey aborted half way to the Red Planet. No illness, but engine malfunction made it necessary to return, and the crew landed back safely on Earth's moon.

Orion-3 encountered no glitches, with its much-improved nuclear propulsion, a well-insulated hull, and a seasoned crew:

two American astronauts and two Russian cosmonauts, four men who would be the first humans on Mars.

Separation of the landing module from the Orion-3 spaceship went smoothly. Shortly after separation, NASA sent a new text message. "Congratulations to our astronauts and cosmonauts. You will make history, the first humans on Mars. Unlike Columbus, you know where you're going."

Family members also sent texts, along with pictures to remind the crew of life back home. Video of the crew showed calm professionals in thick space suits, their faces hidden behind reflective space helmets. Unseen was their anxiety and excitement over being the first.

First, first, first. The word was used so often it became almost a cliché. First would make them world famous, but just getting there safely was the goal—confirming NASA as not just competent but the ultimate Earth space agency.

China had also made a Mars attempt and failed. In 2035, their spaceship blew apart a million miles from Earth. NASA could never learn why but knew the Chinese program was set back, possibly for a decade. Both India and Japan had rovers on Mars but no spaceship capable of carrying people.

At a speed of 15,000 mph, the landing module and its crew of four circled the planet one hundred miles above the surface. Five thousand miles from the Jezero Crater, a prompt appeared on a large screen inside the cabin: Prepare for Module Descent. The landing was pre-programmed, though the crew could override if necessary.

"Looks good," said NASA Captain Scott Kanter. "Everyone ready?"

"Yah," replied cosmonaut Fyodor Dyschenko. "I can't wait to land, to walk again with some gravity. Take me to Mars."

"Agreed," echoed the other two crew members, astronaut Billy Williams and cosmonaut Anton Komarov.

The question of which specific crew member would be the first to step on Mars vexed NASA and Roscosmos, the Russian space agency. They each claimed the right to be first. In what NASA called a brilliant compromise, the landing module was reconfigured to include two parallel ladders, so two men could descend together and put their feet on the ground simultaneously.

The two "firsts" would be astronaut Kanter and cosmonaut Dyschenko. The other two men would descend as the second pair. This moment would of course be transmitted to Earth from cameras in the module, attached to the spacesuits, and in NASA's Perseverance rover near the landing site.

"We're going to feel a little unsteady after three months of no gravity," Kanter reminded his crew close to touching down. "Fortunately, Mars has about two-fifths of Earth's gravity, but it's going to take some adjustment. Everyone, remember to walk slowly."

"To walk upright will be a blessing," replied Williams.

The module parachute deployed, and they rapidly descended toward the Jezero Crater.

"I can see the rovers!" exclaimed Kanter, looking through a port window.

"Great," said Williams. "Hope we don't hit any."

"We won't, but we'll land close to Perseverance. I'm sure Mission Control is watching through the rover's cameras. This is exciting."

"Yah, the whole world is watching," said Dyschenko. "Certainly, all of Russia. I will be hero. First man on Mars."

"Man?" asked Kanter.

"Excuse," said Dyschenko. "First men."

"Hold on," said Kanter to his crew. "We're going to land any second."

Plunk! The module hit the surface.

"We made it! Too bad we can't contact NASA in real time," said Kanter. "I would love to say something memorable, like 'The Eagle has landed.'"

The crew unbuckled from their seats and stood ready to exit. Kanter opened the module door and pressed a button, lowering two short ladders to the ground.

"Are you ready, Fyodor?"

"Ready, captain."

"Let's go." The two men, careful to step together, descended the ladders. Feet on the ground, they gave each other a hug, as well as can be accomplished in bulky space suits. Then came the other two crew.

The four men stood for a moment and surveyed the landscape: red, like a Utah desert but without plants or any life-form. Within a hundred yards or so, they could see three Mars rovers.

"There's the Perseverance rover," said Kanter, pointing to his right. "It's got us on camera, for sure. NASA will see us in about another ten minutes. Let's all wave at the rover and walk over."

"Hello, Houston," said Williams as he waved at the machine.

Mission Control Center - Houston

MCC FLIGHT ENGINEER 1: "Perseverance rover has them in view. Kanter and Dyschenko are coming down together. Perfect." A few minutes later: "The crew appear in good shape. All are waving."

MCC FLIGHT ENGINEER 2: "China and Russia are using different satellite transmissions from their rovers, so they may be a few seconds more or less. But they should be viewing the same scene."

MCC FLIGHT ENGINEER 1: "Well, one view or another, I imagine most of the world not sleeping is watching this historic moment. The first humans on Mars."

———

The Orion crew began walking toward Perseverance. Just then, they saw four human-sized spacesuits coming from behind another rover and walking in their direction.

"What is that?" asked Kanter. "Robots dressed in spacesuits? What the hell?"

The four spacesuits, faces hidden by helmets, continued walking toward the NASA crew, stopping just ten meters away.

"Scott," exclaimed Williams, "I don't think those are robots!"

"Apparently not," mumbled Kanter.

"People!" exclaimed Dyschenko. "People on Mars before us! How possible?"

One of the spacesuits carried a folded canvas. With the aid of a companion, the cloth was unfolded into a large rectangle, three-by-six feet. One-half of the canvas showed a bright-red national flag with five yellow stars in the flag's upper left corner. The other half contained a message in large print, written in English, Chinese, and Cyrillic. The spacesuits slowly rotated the canvas so the flag and its message could be transmitted by all rovers in the area.

The Republic of China Welcomes NASA to Mars.

The Brother Who Never Was

by Meredith Martin

Emily absentmindedly fingered the edge of the yellowed photograph. It had been cut in half with a decisive swipe of scissors. Part of Grandfather Scott's left shoulder was missing. The part remaining showed an elegantly dressed, balding, middle-aged man holding the hand of a small waif-like girl with sorrowful brown eyes—her mother. It was their only picture of her grandfather. He had been a doctor. She wanted to learn as much as possible about this mysterious man who died when her mother was ten years old.

The plane touched down at the airport in Green Bay, Wisconsin. If the weather held out, she could drive to Hurley by late afternoon. It was an easy two hours on US Highway 141 North.

For the first hour, Emily kept going over in her mind what her mother, Anna, told her about the picture. It was faded and creased through years of being lovingly handled. Anna said she did not know who was on the other half of the picture. She thought perhaps it was her mother. After their divorce, Grandmother burned all pictures of Grandfather Scott. Somehow, this one had escaped her wrath. Emily was on a mission to find out all that she could about her grandfather and this picture.

The sky had turned from a swirly gray to an ominous charcoal, beckoning like the maw of a cave. Emily tuned the radio to the weather channel. A traveler's alert was being broadcast. A blizzard was being predicted for northern Wisconsin and Michigan. Travelers were warned of up to two feet of snow and icy conditions. People were warned to stay home.

Oh well, she mused, *I will be there soon.* She kept on driving.

Thirty minutes later, heaven released its fury. Fat, wind-driven snowflakes piled up on her windshield faster than her wipers could dispose of them. The road looked like a white strip through an abandoned countryside. It took all of her strength to keep the howling gusts from tossing her car off the road like a Matchbox toy. Thoughts of getting to Hurley were replaced by *I have to find a hotel now!*

Time seemed as frozen as the weather. After struggling for another ten miles, a sign, capped with drifting and sloping snow, peeked through the storm: Roxie's Place, One Mile, Right on Jefferson Ave.

She swung onto Jefferson, tires sliding on hidden ice. She smiled in relief as Roxie's Place loomed up. It looked like an old white German farmhouse with a big, wide porch. Welcoming windows glowed with soft-yellow light. Snow mounds, presumably guest cars, were snug up to it like little chicks to a mother hen.

Arms aching, she plodded in. Behind the desk, a little guy with a generous nose and large ears looked up. Cigarette smoke circled around him like a gauze curtain.

"Help you?" he asked.

"I need a room," Emily said. "Do you have any left?"

"I only got one. It's a bit on the pricey side . . ."

"I'll take it."

"Don't you want to know what it costs first? It's fifty a night—includes breakfast."

"Great. I'll take it."

With a wry smile, he handed Emily a big, old-fashioned key with a metal tag imprinted with the number 13.

"Second floor, all the way to the end. It's kind of a suite. Got a fireplace and everything. Pay when you leave."

What was that all about? Emily wondered as she fitted the key into the lock. She pushed the door open and was assailed with the scent of earthly spice mixed with tobacco. *Whoa, wrong room!* Emily thought as she started to back out.

"Come on in, honey. I've been waiting for you," a husky voice murmured. "You're in the right room. I like to personally welcome all my guests. I'm Roxie, and this is my hotel."

Emily squinted through the soft light to see a buxomly beautiful lady sitting in a royal- blue velvet chair next to a crackling fire. Her long, auburn hair was piled high on her head with wispy tresses trailing carelessly down her face. She wore a pale-blue gown which framed her perfect bosom. She took a puff from a cigarette held in a jeweled holder and said, "You look tired. Come on over here by the fire; I have a brandy for you."

"How did you know . . .?"

"I make it a point to know all about my guests: When they are coming. What they like to drink, and what they are looking for. Your grandfather's picture. I knew your grandfather. He and your mother lived here after the divorce. He was like a rudderless ship drifting through life. But then he met Frances. They fell in love and were married in this hotel. Later they had a son, Paul. It was Frances and baby Paul in the picture.

"But mother said she didn't know who it was."

"After Paul was born, your grandfather bought a house. Your mother was sent away to boarding school. Her father died a year later. Your mother felt abandoned and blamed Frances and Paul."

"Why didn't she tell me?"

"Some things are too painful to acknowledge, because if you do, they become true. To Anna, the only way to continue to believe her father loved her was to pretend that Frances and Paul did not exist. She cut them out of the picture and her life. If she admitted their existence, she must also admit she always doubted her father's love."

"What do I tell her," Emily asked?

"That, only you can decide."

With a weary sigh, Emily sank down into the chair. She took a sip of her brandy. Absorbed in thought, she contemplated this strange turn of events. It had been an exhaustive search, but her mother's secret was safe. She was going to tell her she was not able to find out who was on the other half of the picture. Maybe somethings, even brothers, were best not found.

She did not know when she fell asleep, but she woke in a cheery single room. There was no fireplace—no blue velvet chair. She dressed and made her way to the lobby which looked quite different in the morning light.

"I'm Emily Pearson, room thirteen—I need to pay."

"There is no room thirteen," said a younger version of last night's clerk.

"I was in it, second floor, on the end."

"Miss Pearson, we have not had a room thirteen since the original Roxie's Place burned down thirty years ago. That was Roxie's private room. She died three years before the hotel burned. Only thing saved was her portrait there," he said, pointing up to a picture on the wall in back of the counter.

Emily looked up into Roxie's eyes. She could swear she winked.

The Marker

by Robert E. Marvin

John Danzeg lived in the small village of Hobart, just south of Lima, Ohio. His neighbors described him as a practical man, not given to fanciful thinking. But there he stood, in the old cemetery just outside of town, on a Saturday morning looking at a wooden grave marker he couldn't even read. Again and again, he had visited it without any idea why.

Tufts of crabgrass fluttered in the breeze. He saw cracks forged by the freezing and thawing of so many snows, the holes bored by long dead beetles, and a glossy spiderweb engineered into the largest of the cracks near the ground on its right side.

———

The old man's hands were gnarled and stamped through with the evidence of his hard life. Small nicks and scars peppered the spaces between the wrinkles and the larger scars. He pushed and twisted the blade of his pocket knife in an attempt to widen one of the letters he was carving.

The fading light would soon lead to the darkness that would force him to stop and go back into his small log house. He would not bathe nor undress but simply lie down on the straw mat and cover himself with his one ragged wool blanket. In the morning, he would return to his work.

———

At first, John had stopped to look at two large marble monuments that stood just inside the front gate. Tall and beautiful, each had a six-sided Georgia marble base that held a column of red granite.

John had paused a minute before he made his way to the small, undistinguished looking wooden marker hidden among the weeds at the back corner of the churchyard. He ran his hands across the top, then its face. He felt the worn-away ridges that had once been letters and tried to make out with his touch what he couldn't with his eyes.

———

The old man woke early the next day, stiff and sore. It made getting up difficult. He rekindled the fire and fixed himself a pot of coffee and a slice of stale bread. He looked down at his injured hand. He flexed his fingers. Satisfied it worked well enough, he finished the last of the coffee and walked outside.

He sat down on a small three-cornered stool near the doorway. He had made the stool from a tree he planted behind the log house. It came with him from Pennsylvania, when he brought his five children west after their mother died of the fever.

The tree lived only fifteen years, but it had grown well enough to yield sufficient wood for the stool, for the table inside, and a little more. It was a piece of it he now carved. It had slowly air dried in the rafters above the fireplace, and it was stone hard. It had taken so much effort to fashion the first short word that he wondered if he had enough strength left in his old body to finish the job.

———

John ran a weary finger across the carving. It was cut deep into the heart of the board. His fingers traveled back and forth across the remains of what had been the first word on the marker. It must have been important to whoever carved it because, after so much wear, its remains were still faintly visible. He could tell there had been six lines carved into the gray wood. Each one contained but a single word. The first letter of the first word had been a *B,* and the first letter in the second line was still recognizable as a *J.* He ran his fingers along each word. There was a $\check{z}$ in the third line, and that word ended in a *G*.

Time and weather had erased so much of the other letters that they were unreadable. Even so, he felt a strange sense of familiarity with them.

The summer sun was hot and had climbed high into the sky when, on the tenth day, he finally finished his carving. The end of his work brought only a dull ache to his soul. All the while the carving had occupied his entire mind, but now the weight of what had happened crushed his spirit. The old man dropped his knife. It disappeared into the marigolds that grew near the porch.

He closed his eyes and leaned back. His arms and back ached. There would be plenty of time for digging the grave, it would be so small. He would have this one last night with the little one.

A breeze caused the candle to flicker. Even though the child was long past hearing the story his grandfather would tell, the old man told it anyway. He sat by the fire, pulled the tiny cradle near, and began. He looked down at the small bundle and spoke in a whisper. He told it of the ocean voyage he had taken to get to this country and of the hope he had felt. He spoke of the beautiful girl he met in New York, of their marriage, and their five children. A far-off sadness clouded his voice as he spoke of her death and his move to the Ohio territory.

He told how he had managed to rear the children, and how they married and moved away. He told it of its aunts and uncles, and of the marriage of its mother and father. Sadness clouded his voice as he told of its mother's death the day it was born, and of its father's grief that had driven him away.

In the end, the old man's voice trailed off, and he stopped mid-sentence. He sat there by the cradle, long after the candle had burned down, and the fire had gone out.

John bent down and pulled the weeds and crabgrass away from the base of the marker. He grasped the top with both hands and straightened it. Then he wedged several field stones against the back to keep it straight. A car crept slowly by. He watched it for a minute, dusted off his hands, and walked to his car to get the flowers.

As the rays of the sun warmed his face, the old man rose from his chair. He carefully picked up the bundle and went outside. He pulled his shovel from its resting place near the front door and stepped off the porch. He walked slowly to the rise near the stump of the tree, placed the bundle on it, and mechanically began digging. After he had finished, he returned for the last time to his log house. He turned and whispered a last goodbye to his beloved little John.

John Danzeg laid the flowers on the grass in front of the marker. The sight of the flowers eased the sadness that had overtaken him. Another day, even though he didn't know why, he would bring more flowers. He thought he might even plant some there this fall. Maybe marigolds. He had always liked marigolds.

Rocky and the Green Door #2

by Frank T. Masi

Amanda exited the bus and walked to work at the Treasure Gap, an inner-city secondhand store. Each morning on her way, she witnessed a disheveled, eighty-plus-year-old man shut the big, green door of his dilapidated house. Once a small church for migrant Armenian residents, now the building's paint peeled like a bad sunburn, and its tattered shutters held on for dear life. He pushed and pulled to assure the door was locked. Amanda and the man waved, then went on their ways.

From his shabby appearance, Amanda thought he could benefit from visiting the Treasure Gap to get corduroy slacks and a T-shirt for less than three dollars. With a Midwest winter looming, he could buy a bargain-priced flannel coat. She thought, *One of these mornings I'll speak to him.* But right after his wave, he struggled carrying a canvas bag down the street, bouncing left and right due to his severe limp.

"Who is that man from that ratty old house with the big, gnarled, green door?" Amanda asked a co-worker.

"That's Ol' Rocky. He's lived there since the Armenian Church ran out of members, and they shut it. Rocky put a strong lock on the door to keep people out. Maybe he hides dead bodies or young girls chained up like animals. Who knows?"

"But where does he go every morning? I see him lock his door, then hobble down the street clutching a canvas bag."

"Rocky volunteers at the community center soup kitchen up the street. He serves breakfast to the local homeless, drunks, and druggies. Some look like skeletons ready for a trip to the graveyard. He serves bacon and eggs, muffins, coffee—better than I eat. No one knows much about him. Some say he fell out of favor with his oil-baron father. Others claim he went insane and killed his wife and her young lover when he found them in bed. Who knows? But," she hesitated, "God bless him."

Amanda thought about the old man that night. Maybe it was best if she didn't talk to him. Eccentric old men living in the haunts of a broken-down church were a nightmare waiting to happen. Shades of *Phantom of the Opera*. And what about that brown bag he toted? If he worked at the soup kitchen, why would he bring food? Goosebumps crawled up her arms like spiders when she thought of the macabre things that could result from befriending this Rocky guy. His behavior was a mystery she couldn't shake, so she kept an eye on him, looking for signs of. . .she didn't know what.

Over the next two weeks, Amanda observed something unusual. Each morning, at least twenty-five derelicts waited outside the community center. She noticed they were never the same bunch; only new people showed up in the cold or the rain, hats pulled low, collars yanked up around their necks. One visit, and they disappeared.

This fact scared Amanda. Was Rocky herding them like cattle then slaughtering them? Where would he hide the bodies? What did Rocky carry in the canvas bag—maybe rat poison or arsenic? If Rocky were committing grizzly crimes, she'd have to report them to the police. Amanda had her suspicions. She had no evidence but had an idea how to get it.

One morning after waving to Ol' Rocky from the bus stop, Amanda skipped work and headed to a public restroom. She donned old, torn, faded jeans; a threadbare, coffee-stained T-shirt; a sweater, and a soiled Pittsburgh Pirates cap. Amanda stood in line with the rest of the crowd. Pressed forward when the doors opened, she landed in the all-purpose room with seven card tables set restaurant-style with checkered tablecloths, cutlery, plates, napkins, and coffee mugs. *Well, okay,* she thought. *If a catered breakfast is the way it's done, I'll go with the flow, but I won't eat. I'll pocket some food for evidence and fake nausea or cramps.*

A bell rang. Ol' Rocky popped up in front of the room decked in a chef's hat, white apron, and white gloves backed by long tables piled high with food. He bowed as everyone applauded. Rocky announced he would serve them their final breakfast, because today was the start of a new life for each; this was a coming-out party. "I'm the host," he said in a gravelly voice, "and I'll be your server."

The attendees clapped again. Ol' Rocky bowed, then visited each table, serving eggs and all the fixings from a silver tray, pouring coffee from a carafe.

This whole routine frightened Amanda. What new beginning did he refer to? Why was this a final breakfast, yet a coming-out party? Everyone seemed to know, except her. Fear gripped her, tightening in her chest. What had she gotten herself into? Was this a ritual or a mass suicide? She wanted to run, but it was too late. She came for evidence, but she only had suspicions.

So, she feigned cramps to avoid eating. She grabbed handfuls of eggs and potatoes and shoved them into her pockets, then purposely spilled coffee on her T-shirt, so police forensics could discover poison. The room grew quiet for the next thirty minutes as the diners consumed their breakfasts; some asked for seconds. She heard muffled giggles from a few tables, an unholy sound in this macabre atmosphere.

Then Ol' Rocky appeared up front, rang the bell, and spoke slowly. "Today is the day you start your new life. You're being cared for in the hope that, after today, you'll care for yourself. Lift up your metal dishes, and you'll find what you need taped to the bottom." He smiled, baring a mostly toothless mouth.

Amanda raised her dish and found an envelope taped to the bottom. She ripped it open, saw a pile of bills, and counted the money. "Ten thousand dollars," she whispered to herself. She broke out in a sweat, her tattered T-shirt stuck to her body, and her heart beat so loud she thought she would attract attention. She looked around. Everyone was counting, some very slowly, some with tears streaming down their dirty faces.

She looked up and saw Ol' Rocky, still smiling; but a tear ran down his cheek as he surveyed the reaction of the crowd.

He said, "My good friends, leave this place, never return, and start your new lives. Enjoy the fruits of the world, be productive, and find everlasting love. May you be blessed with plenty until your final days."

Amanda filed out with the others, clutching her envelope. As she passed Ol' Rocky at the door, his eyes lit up.

"I thought you'd visit one day. Please keep this secret in your heart. The disadvantaged come here for a fresh start. Making this public will bring it to a halt. I'll see you in the morning," he said, as he kissed her hand then bounded away folding the canvas bag to haul another day of cash.

Amanda buried the evidence in her heart. No need to report this to the police. Love and kindness were alive and well. She contributed $10,000 to St. Jude's Hospital where impaired children go for a new start.

Who Killed Corker?

by Phyllis McKinley

Father Malloy paused at the nurses' station. St. Joseph's Nursing Home was in its usual late morning flurry of activity. He waited for nurse Beth to finish her phone call and approach him. They both knew Malcom, Beth's ninety-two-year-old father-in-law, was deteriorating.

"Has Carl been in to see him yet?" Father Malloy asked.

Beth detected the urgency in his voice. She shook her head. Since Carl and Beth were married by Father Malloy over thirty years ago, Carl had never made peace with his dad. Beth had tried to persuade him to visit, especially now, before it was too late.

"Malcolm's obviously fading," Father Malloy spoke with the directness of one familiar with the dying, "but he squeezed my hand when I asked if he'd like to receive the last rites. I'll come back this evening to administer the sacrament. Seven o'clock, if you'd like to be there."

Beth nodded, tears in her eyes as she returned to her duties.

Carl sat in his utility truck at the building site where he was the electrical contractor. He hadn't touched his lunch, just lit one cigarette after another. The smoke stung his eyes as he fought back tears. Beth's text told him his dad would be receiving the last rites. Carl hadn't been to church in years, but he knew this ritual signaled the end.

A few hours . . . would his dad even know him? What could they possibly talk about? It was too late for peace now, wasn't it? Carl reasoned with himself as he lit one more cigarette and slowly inhaled.

A truck pulled up beside his; Gary, his boss, hopped out.

"Hey, buddy. You look a mess. What's going on?"

Carl tried to speak.

"Dad. Dying . . ." was all he managed to mutter.

Gary put his arm on Carl's sleeve.

"Listen buddy, we're okay here today. Why don't you just pop over to the home now? You'll feel better after . . . after he's . . . after it's over."

Carl nodded, butted his cigarette, and drove away.

Beth led him gently to Room 202. Carl did not recognize the skeletal ghost in the bed.

"Malcolm," Beth bent close to his ear, "you have a special visitor to see you."

Malcolm's pale eyes flickered toward the door. Beth pulled a chair close and motioned to Carl. She took his strong, weathered hand and rested Malcom's dusky, frail one in it. As Carl clasped his fingers over his father's hand, he could no longer restrain the tears.

"I'll leave now," Beth whispered, tiptoeing out. "If you need me, just ring the call bell."

Carl had arrived with anger and decades of resentment to unload on his dad. Instead, here he was, shaking, and bawling like a child. Malcolm's grip tightened, and Carl saw a tenderness in his eyes that he had never noticed during all those bitter years. The fragile chest heaved with every breath as his dad gathered energy to speak.

"Thank you for coming, Carl. Thank you."

"Oh Dad." Carl sobbed as their eyes met, and it occurred to him that perhaps he had never really looked into his dad's eyes until this moment.

"Oh Dad . . . I'm sorry, so sorry."

"Carl," Malcolm's voice had gained strength, "uncle, I'm not your dad. I'm your uncle."

Carl could hear his heart suddenly thumping in his chest. His hand reached to hold the bed rail as he felt his head spinning.

"What? What are you talking about?"

Malcolm struggled for another deep gasp of air.

"Your real father was Eddie, my older brother Eddie. He was nicknamed 'Corker' by his cronies. He made poor choices. Ran away from home at fourteen. I was only six." Malcolm coughed and wheezed as he uttered the words.

Carl sat speechless. He fumbled for his cigarettes before realizing he could not smoke here, now. He leaned in closer to hear the weak, raspy voice. Malcolm went on.

"So, Eddie came back twenty years later. He was a hardened mess. No one knew where he'd been or what all he'd been into. First night back, he got drunk and rowdy. Bouncer tossed him out of the bar. He picked up a young girl walking home from her late shift at the diner. Raped her."

Carl gasped, as Malcolm closed his eyes, and his breath came in weak flutters. Another coughing spell, face purpled, but Malcolm continued.

"The young girl, Aileen; she had the baby. Named him Carl. But she hemorrhaged and died an hour after she delivered you. Papa 'Corker,' he just disappeared again. We heard he was murdered two or three years later, but no one knows who did it. What he didn't know, being away all those years, was that our momma had another baby after me. A sweet little girl. Aileen. The girl he raped was my baby sister, his own younger sister."

Malcolm's hand tensed inside Carl's.

Carl smothered an oath, wondered if he was hearing this for real, or had he entered some delusional state.

Malcolm's voice trembled as he went on.

"Martha and I decided to adopt you, so you wouldn't end up in an orphanage. We took you in, raised you like our own, as best we could. We loved you; I know we did."

"But . . ." Malcolm paused as if unable, or unwilling, to finish.

"But what, Dad?" Carl leaned in.

"But every time I looked at you, I got angry. Angry at Eddie, angry at what he did to Aileen, angry at you for looking like him.

Not your fault, of course. None of it. So sorry . . . so terribly sorry." Malcolm wept.

Carl felt the hand in his getting cool, limp. He rang the call bell. Before Beth arrived, he raised the thin form and cradled Malcolm in a deep embrace.

"It's okay, Dad. I understand now. It's all okay. I love you, Dad."

Beth arrived as Carl was laying him back on the pillow.

She squeezed Carl's hand and pressed a note into it.

"Here's the number, dear. Please go call Father Malloy and tell him Malcolm no longer needs the last rites."

The funeral was well attended, and Carl gave a touching tribute to his dad. Word of the reconciliation had spread with haste through the small community. After the committal service was over, and the last guests had left the reception, Carl sought out Father Malloy. He had many answers now, but one more question still haunted him.

"Father Malloy, I suspect you are the only one who knows the answer to my question."

"I'll be glad to help you with anything I can, Carl. You've had a rough week. What's on your mind?"

"My dad, er . . . Malcolm, was close to you, Father. He was a devout Catholic. Believed in confession and all that."

"He was a good man, Carl. He truly was."

"So, tell me. Do you know who killed Corker?" Carl scanned the priest's face intently for a response, but Father Malloy never blinked.

"I cannot answer that." He put his arm around Carl's shoulders and gave him a warm smile. "I took a vow. The confessional is the cemetery for secrets."

Forever

by Mark McWaters

T he new waitress went up to the diner's owner and helped her stack coffee cups behind the counter. "Thank you again, Darcy, for the job. Seriously. I know my looks are . . . *challenging* for some people."

"Lindsey, some people don't have the good sense God gave 'em. You served your country and paid a price that'd put most folks in the ground. You survived, hon. *That* tells me a lot. Long as you can do the job, Darcy's Diner has a spot for you. Are we clear, soldier?"

"Ma'am, yes, ma'am!"

The two women chuckled and hugged. "Now, get ready. Pickup from AB Construction just pulled in. Those boys are gonna be hungry. Any of 'em give you a hard time—"

"No worries, Darcy. I've handled lots worse than a tableful of rowdy rednecks."

"God knows you have girl. Grab your pad, and go get 'em."

The group came in loud and laughing like always. But the jokes and good-natured shoving died away when Lindsey walked up.

Darcy rolled napkins behind the counter and watched, holding her breath while Lindsey greeted the men. Several of them gaped openly at her pinned up sleeve and the prosthetic leg below her skirt. The gang boss, three inches taller than his tallest man, with *Magnus* stitched on his blue shirt, stared the longest.

The loudest of the group sniffed and said, "Little lady, how in *hell* you gonna carry four cups of coffee with one arm and a robot leg? Much less four plates of biscuits and gravy and extra grits all around, hm?"

Magnus spun the man around and slapped him hard across the mouth. He had his fist drawn back for round two, when Darcy tossed the pile of napkins aside and started around the counter. She stopped when Lindsey spoke.

"Gentlemen, please? This is my first day, and my boss over there's worried I can't cut it." She tucked her pad under the armpit of her pinned sleeve and snapped her fingers. "Darcy? Napkin?" Darcy threw one her way. Lindsey snagged the rolled linen in midair, pivoted, and tossed it to the man massaging his jaw. Then she walked up to Magnus and pressed his cocked arm down. "No harm, no foul," she whispered.

"Tell you the truth, guys? Our coffee's hot enough to boil crawdads, and I *do* worry about spilling it. So, do me a favor? Don't make any sudden moves? I'd hate to pour a whole tray of hot Joe in someone's lap."

Three of the men gaped from her to their boss. The big man scowled and started to speak. Lindsey silenced him with a finger on his lips. The men's eyes opened even wider while she held it there a full five seconds.

"Now," she turned and faced the group, "who's hungry?"

Darcy exhaled and went to check on the kitchen.

The end of the day came, and only one table had customers. Darcy shut down the grill and filled two glasses with ice and cola. "Come on, Lindsey. My old bones need a rest." She walked off without waiting for an answer. "Corner booth has the softest seats."

Darcy sat on one side. Lindsey braced herself on the table and lowered herself onto the red vinyl across from her. They sat and sipped their sodas. Lindsey rubbed her thigh and grimaced.

"You okay, honey?"

"Yeah, it's just—do you mind? I need to get this thing off."

"Do it. Please. Get comfortable."

"It's not pretty—"

"Hon, if I could take my two barking dogs off, orthopedic shoes and all, you better believe I'd join you."

Lindsey reached down and tugged back and forth. The prosthetic came free with a soft pop. "Whew! God, that feels better than taking my bra off. Mind if I lay it—?"

"Put it right there on the seat beside you, dear, and don't think another thing about it. I reckon it deserves a soft place to rest too. So, tell me, how'd your first day go?"

Lindsey took a deep gulp of soda and stifled a burp. "Started off shaky but, I don't know. *You* tell *me*."

Darcy sipped her cola and burped long and loud. "Truth?"

"Always."

"I *was* worried, at first. Those construction boys can be a challenge. But the way you handled 'em, especially their big boss." She laughed. "I'd say you and him made a *connection*."

Lindsey sipped her cola and said nothing.

"His name's Magnus," Darcy said. "It fits him. Between us girls, I always wondered if it fit him *everywhere*." She raised her eyebrows and giggled. "He showed up wearing an AB Construction shirt about a year ago. A little rough around the edges, but don't we all have edges that need sanding?"

The front door opened, and the bell jangled to announce another visitor.

"Kitchen's closed," Darcy yelled. "What the—?"

Lindsey turned, and the big man from earlier walked up to their table and stopped. He looked at her, then at the titanium leg beside her.

"Magnus?" Darcy said. "Grill's off, dear. I might could find a slice of cherry pie with your name on it."

"Nah, Darcy. I'm fine. I came in for her."

Magnus narrowed his eyes at Lindsey, then stared hard at her sock-covered stump and her prosthesis.

She tugged her empty sleeve straight. "How you doing, sergeant?" she said.

He nodded. "Good to see you, lieutenant."

"Oh, goody," Darcy clapped. "You two have secrets!"

"What do you want?" Lindsey said.

"Mind if I sit?" he said.

"That wouldn't be a good idea."

"Know what?" Darcy said. "Grill back there needs my attention." She stood, and neither of the two looked her way. "Okay, then. Yell if you need me."

"Scoot over," Magnus said.

"What are you doing?"

"What I should have done two years ago. Scoot."

"Stand down, sergeant."

"Army's done with us, lieutenant. I was never all that good following orders anyway, remember?"

She felt heat tickle her neck.

"I'm not leaving, Lindsey."

"Fine. Take a good look." She shoved her leg over on the seat and scooted.

He sat, and she moved farther away when their thighs touched.

"Took you long enough," he said.

She shrugged. "How'd you find me?"

He chuckled. "Records are one thing the army's good at. Your family's here."

"Was here. They're gone." She touched her pinned sleeve. "Like a lot of things."

"Give me your sleeve," he said.

"That's cruel, even for—"

"Your other sleeve."

"No."

He grabbed her wrist and rolled back her sleeve to reveal an elaborate tattoo of tribal spikes and flourishes. He gently stretched her arm out on the table and laid his arm beside hers.

"*No.*" Tears flooded down her cheeks.

He grabbed her chin, forced her to look at him. "*Yes.*"

His arm also had a tattoo. On each, the design looked unremarkable, all random swirls and sharp lines. But, laid side-by-side, the tattoos fit together, and the design became clear. It spelled out one word.

FOREVER.

He put his arm around her shoulders, snuggled her into him, then leaned over and kissed the top of her head. "Yes," he whispered in her hair. "Always and forever, *yes.*"

Montague's Obsession— The Lady in Red

by George August Meier

I read the name on her business card and gasped. She was *the* woman—Montague's obsession. They'd been young lovers. She'd left him, and he could never win her back. My partner and friend Montague was attractive, with a charismatic flare. His aqua eyes and long, blond hair drew the attention of countless gorgeous women, but he had no interest in anyone except her. Whenever we reminisced, the conversation always wandered to her—Rosemarie.

———

She'd entered the gallery late in the afternoon. I'd greeted her, but she gave me a cursory nod, appearing to be looking for someone else. She was middle-aged, wearing a wide-brimmed hat, smart scarf, and tailored dress, all in shades of blue. After scanning the room, she stepped toward a display of paintings, looking like a sommelier selecting wine. Her eyes stalled on *The Lady in Red*, a large oil. The only piece not for sale.

She pointed to it. "I want that painting." The painting featured a nude woman sitting on a stool, her neck adorned with a red scarf.

"Did you see the sign?" I asked. "It's for display only."

"Yes," she said, with a hint of a snarl. "But I believe for the right price, anything's for sale."

Although stylishly dressed, she had harsh features, and a demeanor to match. I copied her frosty tone. "I don't think the painter will sell it. He's turned down several offers."

She frowned. "The painter is Lucas Montague, correct?" Without waiting for an answer, she said, "Is he here today?"

"That's the artist. But, he's out of town."

"Who are you?"

"Emory, the gallery manager."

"Well, Emory, tell Monty I came by and want that painting." She handed me her card and marched out.

Her visit needed to be relayed to Montague in person. Early the next day, I drove to the countryside. It was wildflower season, and he had his favorite spot.

His easel was set up in a valley, its converging slopes covered in clusters of red, yellow, and orange. On a distant hillside of dark-green foliage, there were thousands of brilliant-white flowers, appearing as stars against the heavens. Montague's canvas mirrored these images, but more magically.

His brush was kissing the canvas as I came up behind him. Without looking away from the wet paint, he said, "So, what's so important to bring you out to my humble workshop?"

After I handed him the card, he packed up his easel, palate, and paints. I told of the encounter at the gallery as we walked on a dirt path toward our vehicles. He requested I carry the painting and his duffel bag. He called her.

His speech was stuttered, which was unlike Montague. They agreed to discuss the painting over dinner.

He was silent after the call. I made eye contact and raised my brows.

"She's in town on business," he began. "Saw my name on the gallery and came in to say hello. *The Lady in Red* caught her eye."

He asked me to describe her. I had to be careful. I didn't find her beautiful, the way he'd always portrayed her. I described how beautifully she was dressed.

"She's angelic, yes?" he asked.

"In a way, yes."

"In a way? In a way? Your beady eyes are blind."

"My eyes aren't beady."

He scoffed. "You forget, I am a creator. I can give you beady eyes in my world of paint on canvas."

The dinner was to be at Pierre's, a chic restaurant. He came by the gallery on his way, wearing a guayabera shirt and white linen pants, carrying a dozen roses and a folder.

He apologized to me and spontaneously vowed to never paint me with beady eyes.

He said, "I've never told you this. When twenty, I was living on the street and became deathly ill. An angel took me in. My fever was Dante's *Inferno*. She bathed me in ice and her warm kindness. While I was delirious, the angel's face came to me, and her lips caressed my forehead. Love was born. That angel was Rosemarie."

"How long were you together?"

"One glorious year."

"And?" I asked.

"After three months, she was expecting. We celebrated and toasted Fortuna. But we lost the baby in childbirth. My angel's chemistry changed from sweet to sour. And then she was gone."

I gave him a look of commiseration.

"Many times, I've tried to be an alchemist to change her back to the way she was. I've always failed."

I felt bad for Montague but had to say, "Please don't sell her the painting. You've said you lose all inspiration to paint if you don't see it every day."

The following morning, Montague requested I prepare *The Lady in Red* for shipping to Rosemarie.

He stared at it one last time.

"Emory, when she first left me, I feared my heart would cease to spark. I kept listening for the final thump. And now that heart greets me with an ache every new day." He raised his hands high and shouted. "Her presence ignited hope!"

I nodded.

"After presenting the roses, I showed her pictures of us together while we were young." He choked on the last few words. "I again proclaimed my love. And damn her, she said, 'What about the painting?'"

Montague collapsed into a chair and bellowed like a mortally wounded animal. His contorted face fell into his hands. He moaned and then wept for a long time. With eyes shut, he fell silent. I put a hand on his shoulder. He looked up and said, "The torment's been long, hard, and now unbearable. But those four words, 'What about the painting?' they've set me free. For me, Rosemarie is dead. I shall find refuge in my mistress of pigment and cloth."

That afternoon, I advised Montague the painting had been sent. "What price did you agree on?" I asked.

"The only price I was capable of asking—nothing."

"But what about losing your inspiration?"

"Let me worry about that," he said.

"Did she say why she wanted it so badly?"

"She didn't have to. I knew why—it's a portrait of her. As she put it, she didn't want her breasts on display. She reminded me that, when she modeled for it, I promised to keep it a secret."

———

The sun seemed brighter the next morning, as did Montague. The gallery had the familiar smell of fresh oil paint. And there it was. In place of *The Lady in Red* was a new nude wearing only a scarf, with the woman's back facing forward, and a more mature face peeking over a shoulder.

"Her?" I asked.

"Yes. I painted all night."

"What if she someday wants it, too?"

"As I said in the valley, I'm a creator. Her image is etched here." He pointed to his head. "I can create unlimited paintings of her. That's our secret."

He gestured toward the piece and said, "Look closely."

I did and noticed the scarf was blue.

Montague smiled. "I present to you, *The Lady in Blue*. In my world of paint and canvas, I will always have the sweet Rosemarie."

American in Paris

by Barbara Meyers

When the door opened, Philipe arranged his expression into one of wide-eyed appreciation. Bea's answering smile told him he'd succeeded.

He took her hand and twirled her around. "You look lovely, as always. I especially like the scarf. Very *parisienne*."

If possible, her smile grew even wider. "Thank you."

He glanced over her shoulder. "Your friend is not joining us?"

Bea's joy dropped a notch. "No. She's gone to visit l'Orangerie. I hope you don't mind."

"Not at all." He lowered his voice and leaned forward. "I much prefer having *you* all to myself."

Bea giggled like a nervous schoolgirl.

American women were such easy targets. Outwardly they seemed to have so much, but inside so many of them were empty. Easy pickings for someone like him who gave them the attention they so desperately wanted. The excitement of something a bit illicit. A romantic fling during their time abroad with a man they'd never see again.

That's what they all thought anyway. And they were right about one thing. By the time they parted ways, not only would they never see him again, but they also wouldn't see anything else again either.

On the sidewalk, he tucked Bea's hand into the crook of his elbow and patted her fingers. "We'll go to the Parc Monceau, first. It is beautiful there. Almost as beautiful as you." He glanced at her, admiration in his eyes, to see her blush at the compliment. Gullible American women made such perfect victims. He'd eyed her in a local café two days ago, making sure she noticed him. The next evening, he positioned himself at an outdoor restaurant table across the street from the one where she and her friend were dining. It wasn't hard to make eye contact with her again. She then marched over to him and introduced herself. He had her pegged immediately: A lonely American woman looking for some excitement, some romance. Not getting any from the husband at home.

Beatrice had no shame, for she'd worn her wedding rings today. She'd dressed for him in a matching skirt and jacket and added a scarf by one of his favorite designers. If she only knew how that single accessory teased his imagination with what was to come.

Philipe debated about taking the metro. So many cameras. But Bea would think it odd if they didn't. And, after finding the perfect prey, he didn't want to scare her off. Besides, he could change his appearance easily. Hair dye. Glasses. A beard. A cane.

He ignored the newsstand they passed with its daily papers sporting two-inch headlines. SERIAL KILLER STILL AT LARGE! TOURIST STRANGLER CLAIMS SIXTH VICTIM.

He'd read the articles online earlier. A foreign woman found dead like all the others. No suspects. No leads. Ah, sweet Marie. In Paris on business. Not quite as pliable as the Americans. He imagined her body shipped back to Switzerland sans her pearl necklace. She should have re-thought that second drink with a stranger at the hotel bar.

He let Bea babble during the train ride, while he pretended to listen. Philipe made all the right mono-syllabic responses in all the right places, encouraging her to tell him more when in truth he had no idea what she was saying. Something about husbands who refused to travel to Paris and her long friendship with Mary, who'd chosen yet another museum over a visit to the gardens.

Thank you, Mary. What will you do when your little lamb doesn't come home?

They spent a couple of hours wandering around the garden, and Philipe wasn't surprised when Bea admitted she wasn't used to so much exercise. He suggested refreshments at a café where he could secure her agreement to join him somewhere more private.

Over glasses of mediocre pinot noir, Bea made a surprising confession. "I asked my husband to join me here in Paris."

Philipe didn't have to feign surprise. Perhaps he'd have to rethink—

Tears shimmered in Bea's eyes. "He said no. I knew he would."

Recovering quickly, Philipe reached for her hand, rubbing his thumb gently over the back of it. "My dear, Bea. I am afraid your husband is blind. I do not know what to make of a man who does not want to spend time with his beautiful wife in the most beautiful city in the world."

He handed her a napkin to blot her tears. "I, on the other hand, would be honored to spend more time with you. Perhaps you would even grant me *temps privé*."

"What do you mean?"

He kept himself from scoffing at her pretend innocence. Like most American tourists, she couldn't be bothered to learn the most basic of French phrases. "You. Me. Alone. Together. Where the only thing you're wearing is that scarf that's been driving me crazy with desire all afternoon."

"Philipe, I don't know. Are you serious?"

"Deadly serious. Isn't romance what you want? A—how do you say? A fling? Before you go back to your life in America?"

He saw her uncertainty. Interest warring with caution. He wouldn't push. He wouldn't insist or coerce. He would wait for her decision, while fantasies of her scarf wrapped around her neck tighter and tighter—

"Yes, it's what I wanted." She bit her lip. "But I'm not . . . you might want to leave some of my clothes on."

He laughed. So insecure, his Bea. Too much American bread. Too many chocolates trying to fill that hole inside her. His excitement grew.

He leaned across the table. "I know a place near here. We'll be completely alone."

"Let's go."

He led her to a deserted house undergoing extensive renovations. He doubted Bea knew that today was *Fête du Travail*. The workers were probably spending the holiday demonstrating somewhere. He'd picked the lock earlier, certain of Bea's acquiescence. "It belongs to a friend who's traveling," he lied. "He won't mind that we're here."

He led her to a bedroom where the remodeling hadn't yet begun.

"Bea," he whispered, beginning his practiced seduction.

"Yes," she said. She kept repeating that one word until all her clothes were gone except for her scarf, which Philipe playfully wrapped around her neck. He pulled the ends tighter and tighter, watching in excited satisfaction as her eyes bulged in disbelief, and her body bucked beneath him.

"Yes, Bea, yes. Just what you wanted. What you needed."

He'd keep the scarf as a souvenir, he decided. Why not? Bea had been special to him, in her own way, for a short time.

Her phone buzzed from inside her purse. Using the scarf to cover his hand, he pulled it out to see she had a text message from the husband she'd mentioned earlier. *Surprise sweetheart! Changed my mind. I'll be there tomorrow morning. I love you.*

Genuinely amused for the second time that day, Philipe thought for a moment before he texted back. *Wonderful,* mon chéri. *I'm dying to see you.*

He folded the scarf into a neat square and tucked it into his pocket, straightened his clothing, and bid Bea adieu.

The Empty Chair

by Joanna Michaels

Memories of Sarah fill my Sunday afternoon as I sit beneath the canvas roof of our favorite place on the beach—a little tiki bar called Jamaica Johnny's. My sun-warmed skin cools, as palm fronds feather-dance against a darkening sky, and rain etches circles in the sand. I sit alone, sipping rum and Coke, as lightning strikes in the distance. The pounding beat of a reggae band silences the thunder. The chair to my left is empty. Sarah's chair. I summon a vision of her wind-tousled hair, a half-smile playing on her lips. The reggae beat is sensual; the song suggestive with lyrics about how the singer wants to make their girl sweat.

I close my eyes and will myself to see her, as I did that other rainy Sunday when we sat here together; her fingers reaching across the table, pressing into the palm of my hand. We listened to the reggae beat, the same singer singing how they want to make their girl sweat.

I remember how captivated I was the first time I saw her at David's party. He brought me into the family room to show off an art deco sculpture he had purchased from a Sarasota gallery. Sarah stood a few feet from the sculpture, talking with a small group of women, hands in her pockets, laughing. The round tortoiseshell glasses she wore had slipped down to the end of her nose, but she didn't seem to notice. The sight enchanted me.

"David," I murmured, tugging on his sleeve. "Who is the blonde wearing the khaki overalls?"

"That's Sarah," he said. "She's new in town."

I asked if she was there alone and if she was single. David told me I should ask her myself and dragged me over to the women.

"Excuse me, ladies," he announced in his drama-queen voice. "I have an important introduction to make." He grasped Sarah's left hand. "Sarah, I'd like you to meet my dear friend Rebecca."

She smiled. A crooked, brief smile that was adorable. I know that sounds corny, but it's true. Then David placed my right hand into Sarah's left hand, so that we were not shaking hands but holding hands. I felt my cheeks warm when he pressed our palms together and said, "Stay," as if he were commanding a dog. Then he turned and sauntered away. Sarah and I both laughed self-consciously, and as much as I hated to do it, I released her hand.

Two things I never believed in were love at first sight, and happily ever-after. But meeting Sarah changed my mind. Within the first nine months of dating, we committed to each other. I dreamed of someday marrying Sarah, if such a thing ever became possible. Yet we never even lived together. When I proposed the idea to her, she reminded me she wasn't out to her family and may never be.

Sarah's parents are Christians with a capital *C*—Southern Baptists who consider homosexuality a sin. Even worse, her brothers believe being gay is an abomination, which caused Sarah to fear being cut off from her nieces. Sarah's sexuality had to remain a secret, and that secret forced me back into the closet with her.

For the next year and a half, we kept separate homes. And then the unthinkable happened. A malignant brain tumor struck Sarah down. Of course, I wanted to be with her at every stage, to support her, to let her know I loved her, but her family shut me out. I had always suspected Sarah's mother disliked me—that she could sense Sarah and I shared a secret relationship.

The night before her surgery, I found Sarah alone in her hospital room, sitting on the edge of the bed, barefoot and wearing a blue hospital gown. When I leaned over to kiss her, she turned her face, and offered me her cheek.

"Mother is here somewhere," she whispered.

"Okay." I perched next to her on the bed. "Your teeth are chattering. Where's your robe? You should have socks on."

"Not cold," she said, her chin quivering. "Scared."

I grabbed her hand. "Oh, Sarah, I—"

Before I finished my sentence, her mother bustled into the room. "Well, hello, Rebecca. How long have you been here?" Sarah pulled her hand out from under mine. "You know, dear, it's not proper to sit on a patient's hospital bed."

"I'm sorry," I said, my cheeks burning. "I just got here a couple of minutes ago."

Sarah told her mother she was okay with me sitting there, but I stood and moved to the foot of the bed.

"Get under the covers, Sarah." Her mother dimmed the lights and gestured to the door. "She needs her rest now."

Sarah's eyes pleaded with me to stay. I wish I hadn't given in to her mother's obvious command that I leave, but I did. I leaned over, brushed Sarah's forehead with my lips, and whispered, "I love you."

Many months have gone by, and I've returned to Jamaica Johnny's alone, to sit near the beach to close my eyes against the images of hospital sheets soiled with bodily fluids, the silent blip of Sarah's heart monitor arcing and falling in syncopated rhythms. I struggle to erase the hospital scene and instead try to hold on to the memory of Sarah and me making love against a backdrop of the reggae beat. I long for her breath on my cheek, to press my mouth against her throat, and feel the vibration of her life force. My darling, blue-eyed Sarah. The reggae band stops playing, but the song about how I want to make Sarah sweat continues in my head.

The Secret Garden #9

by Joan Wright Mularz

"Where is that child? There's planting to be done!"
I hear Pa's voice and know I don't have much time.

Darn! The buds of so many ideas are in my head, and I want to put them down on paper before I forget them.

I scribble as fast as I can, then run downstairs before he can come after me. Pa has no patience for anything that doesn't increase farm production, and spending working hours dreaming up ideas riles him more than anything.

I skid to a halt in the kitchen. "What took you so long, Caleb?"

I gulp down some orange juice to delay my answer. "I was thinking about growing my garden someday, Pa."

A smile of satisfaction slips over his face as he takes a sip of his coffee. "With that kind of initiative, you'll be a good farmer someday." He finishes off his last mouthful and adds, "Eat your breakfast, son, then meet me in the field. If we work fast enough, maybe we'll have enough time to start you on your own plot today."

As I pour some cereal into my bowl, his springy steps are visible through the screened doorway.

He's buoyant, and I'm deflated. I've added to my physical labor today by misleading him.

It wasn't a lie because I do want a garden, except I want it full of stories made by cultivating ideas.

I want my seedling thoughts to blossom into spectacular novels.

How do I explain that to a man who sees value only in acquiring skills to make fallow land produce a good harvest . . . who views my desire to write as "peculiar"?

I add milk to my cereal, take in a big spoonful, and listen to the crunching as it reverberates in my skull.

Somewhere inside that cavity is my brain yearning to be exercised. I wish farming allowed me more think breaks.

I'm soon lost in the mind-numbing and backbreaking work growing vegetables requires. My thoughts are on how hot I am and how much my legs and arms ache, but I also worry.

Will Pa still think my writing is unimportant when I'm a man and doing what I love?

If I keep hiding my true passion until I'm old enough to make my own decisions, will I still be capable of creating stories?

Will my brain stop producing because my ability is receiving so little support now? Mind gardens need maintenance just like farms— the compost of shared ideas through discussions and accessible books, sunlight shed by acknowledgment and validation, and even the rain of challenges to spur new ways of thinking.

When lunchtime arrives, I follow Pa and his hired workers to the picnic tables where Ma has brought out food. Before I even get there, my nose tells me today's sandwiches are filled with slow-cooked shredded beef, my favorite.

After I help myself to two, I slip away from the group as usual and sit on the grass in the shade of a tree. It's my secret plotting time. Ideas pop up and grow in the fertile soil of my brain, as I create an imaginary landscape and quirky characters to remember for later.

Before bedtime, I'll put them in writing and do some revision.

In the privacy of my room, I'll weed out the rambling passages, pinch back unnecessary words, graft new twists into the plot, and see how it blooms.

At the end of the planting day, I stop for a look over the land. It's good stuff, rich loam and, with luck, the harvest will be fruitful. I think about Dad. *His life is rooted in this place. Not mine. I want to branch out.*

For now, my life is like container gardening: one pot for the farm and Dad, and one pot for the stories and me. I mulch and irrigate both, but my dream is for my secret story pot to overflow and produce rhizomes that create annual beauties and perennial favorites that will make me proud and inspire other kids to follow their secret dream.

Grandpop's Trunk

by Christopher Myers

James Jones Sr. held his wife's hand tightly, as the winter sun disappeared on Nassau Street in Princeton, New Jersey. She knew he was ready for his cocktail, and their shopping bags from Brooks Brothers were beginning to feel heavy. Each monthly visit ended in the Nassau Tavern on Palmer Square with a bourbon Old-Fashioned, escargot, and prime rib.

After their meal, James and Antoinette took the train from Princeton to Penn Station in New York. James wore his masculine Harris Tweed suit under a gray Chesterfield overcoat. His diagonal blue-and-red striped repp tie remained tightly tied in the crisp white shirt's buttoned collar. His tanned skin glowed from their recent trip to the pink beaches and soothing aquamarine waters of Bimini. They were delighted that evening with outstanding performances on Broadway by Julie Andrews as Guinevere and Richard Burton as King Arthur in Camelot.

Back in Lakewood, New Jersey, Jim, and Toni, as their intimates called them, ran a law practice. Toni was the paralegal and loved Jim. Together they raised James Jr., Linda, and Mary in middle-class comfort, but comfort only lasts a season. The Jones family of Lakewood entered a new season overnight.

Linda, out with her boyfriend, did not come home. His car smashed into a tree, and both were killed instantly. The grief overcame Jim, who responded with more cocktails than were good for him. Toni did her best. Mary started smoking. James Jr. enlisted in the marine corps.

A decade later in Oceanside, California, I was born. No one seemed to mind I had clubfoot; the military hospital reassured my parents Judy and Jay, as James Jr. was now called, that the deformity manifested as a generational backlash. The hurts and disappointments harbored within my ancestors needed an outlet. But grief transformed from deformity into resilience. I developed a personality to survive. I wasn't the sum of braces and scars; I was a Jones.

Grandpop Jim doted over me, despite his inability to speak—the result of a massive stroke. The image of his broad smile on his large, tanned Irish face fueled me, not with pity, but with an ancestor's acceptance and love. He and Grandmom flew cross-country for my christening at the Mission San Luis Rey. He wore a crisp and cool seersucker suit. The stripes played with the vibrant Mediterranean decor of the small chapel, subconsciously planting a style seed in me.

As a teen in Ocean City, Maryland, I attended prep school. I was entering the season where girls held the keys to my self-worth. Mom and Dad could not decipher why I said no to parties. I had an undetected fashion crisis. They were out of touch. Mom rode her horse most days, and her clothes were stable-friendly. Dad spent the day behind cash registers and then went surf fishing until dinner time. My afterschool clothes were out-of-style hand-me-downs and fashion-unconscious purchases from Dollar General and Sears.

My personality took the place of money, travel, and clothes to find acceptance amongst my peers. I labored under the hardships of family businesses that made enough to pay bills and little else. Asking for new clothes just meant another trip to Dollar General. I was resigned to seeing friends at school and the beach, no parties.

Then my classmate Amy invited me to an impromptu party while her mom was away. Not a big party, because it was a small condo overlooking the ocean. This was going to be an up close and personal inspection. I was excited and eager to impress. Sadly, no matter how many times I looked through my closet nothing, nothing, nothing was suitable to wear. I was sunk.

I reluctantly looked through my father's wardrobe and discovered a Brooks Brothers blue blazer. The idea of wearing a blazer in summertime seemed extreme. *Now what?* I looked at the trunk at the end of Mom and Dad's bed. *I wonder what's in there.*

The handsome cedar trunk looked like a smooth bench. I'd seen it a hundred times and never thought about it. It was just part of Mom and Dad's personal landscape. I reached to grasp the lid which was solidly shut. It overhung the flush mount lock, which I prayed wasn't locked. I pulled, and the resistant lock open. *When was the last time someone opened this?*

The smell of mothballs filled my nostrils as folded clothes in plastic bags came into my view. *Clothes!* A paisley print caught my eye. I lifted it out. *Can this be true? It's a real 1960s cool-dude smoking jacket!* I set it aside, and my heartbeat began to race when I saw the cream of the crop just beneath a wool scarf: A pile of neatly folded pinstripe Brooks Brothers button-collared shirts. *They fit!* I pulled the winter clothes out of the way. A Chesterfield, a Harris Tweed suit, scarves, and then . . ..*Are those khakis?* Nervous that the khakis were something else, I stalled, examining the label on the inner lining of the Harris Tweed jacket: Made Exclusively for James J. Jones Sr.

Grandpop has come to my rescue! I felt sure Grandpop intended for me to discover this secret. I felt reconnected with him as I reveled at this incredible timeless wardrobe. Grandpop's surprise reintroduced me to his joyful outlook. I was wearing his style, the style of a bon vivant who knew, "Clothes make the man." I walked proudly into Amy's wearing freshly ironed khakis, a blue cloth belt, a red-and-white pinstripe shirt, and my school loafers without socks.

I mingled with about twenty other classmates and felt confident. Without the familiar self-consciousness of not fitting in, my conversation skills ignited laughter and spontaneous input from those within earshot. It was thrilling, like riding a wave. Nobody cared what I wore, except me. I felt the good vibrations giving me contagious ease.

Was it the look of the clothes, the feel of the soft cotton, or the generational bond that lifted my spirit? In retrospect, I believe it was the immense gratitude I felt. In one moment, my need had been met beyond anything I could have imagined. Naturally, I was thrilled.

The dividend, the lifelong gift that has lasted, long since those clothes became threadbare, and still bears fruit: Grandpop had revealed the secret of style.

The Hearing:

Inspired by a True Event
by Mark H. Newhouse

"You are Svetlana Viscanova?" I asked the middle-aged woman standing stiffly in the witness box.

"I am."

"You witnessed the alleged act—"

"I reported it as ordered," the petite, gray-haired woman interrupted.

"Ordered?"

"It is against the law to say anything against our brave forces—"

"This 'law' was only passed last year. Before that, would it have been a crime for a—"

"Objection! The age of the law is irrelevant. It is the law."

The judge sustained Prosecutor Miklovski's objection. "Move on, Rogoff. We want this finished expeditiously." His eyes shot to the rear of the courtroom.

I knew this case was lost before I entered the courtroom in Yefremov. I hoped the people in this rural village would protest. They were afraid. I was as well. "As a teacher, you felt it was your duty to report a child's drawing?"

"I reported it to the headmistress."

"What happened next?"

"She called the police."

"You did not call?"

The prosecutor sounded bored. "Answered."

"We must hear it from her lips," I said. "We are entitled to a defense."

Judge Orlov said, "Speed it up. This is not a homicide."

I nodded. "You did not call the police?"

"It did not occur to me—"

"Because this was not a serious crime?"

"Objection! That we are in court attests to the offense's gravity."

The judge addressed the witness, "It is punishable for teachers to not report such crimes to the authorities—"

"I reported to my superior, sir."

"And what if your headmistress did nothing?" The judge glared at the teacher.

"I never considered she would call the police."

Did I detect regret? "So, when you reported to your headmistress, you assumed she would handle this situation, as she does for minor disciplinary issues. Yes?"

"Objection! An insult to our brave soldiers fighting the enemy threatening our existence is not some minor disciplinary issue—"

"Nonsense! It is a child's drawing. Our constitution protects free speech."

The judge's gavel struck hard. "Do not bring freedom of speech into this. We are in a battle for survival. Insults against our leader and our Special Military Operation cannot be condoned." He leaned toward me. "You will stick to the facts of this case only or face prison yourself."

Shaken, I tried another approach, again wishing I had not been assigned to this case. "The drawing. What struck you about it?"

The teacher aimed bloodshot eyes at Maria, the defendant. "Our great nation's flag with missiles aimed at a mother and child . . . disgraceful."

"The drawing or the reality?"

"Rogoff!" The judge aimed his gavel at me. "Final warning."

"I apologize." I held Maria's drawing up to the witness. "Please identify this flag positioned by the mother and child—"

"Objection! We cannot dignify our enemy's name."

"Sustained. We do not recognize this enemy as other than a rebellious limb of the motherland."

"Yes, Your Honor." I needed to try something else. "Did Maria draw this at home?"

"In class."

"Was it in response to a question . . . an assignment?"

"I . . . I may have been discussing the war—"

"Special Military Operation," the Judge corrected.

"Did you ask the children for opinions of the Special Military Operation?"

"Objection! A teacher would not elicit illegal opinions from children."

The judge appraised the witness. "Did you require students to illustrate their opinions of the Special Operation?"

"No! I would never do that, Your Honor. Never."

The judge sighed. "I see no purpose to this. The witness is dismissed."

I was stunned. "Your Honor, I'm not done—"

"The obscene drawing speaks for itself. It is the best evidence. Do you disagree?"

"They could be crayons," I said, pointing to the three alleged missiles.

The few spectators laughed but quickly quieted under Orlov's withering stare.

"I will not dignify your ludicrous statement with a response," Orlov said. "I will now render my verdict."

"Your Honor, may I call Maria's father?"

"He was found guilty of illegal social media postings and is a fugitive."

Maria did not react. Did she know her father fled?

"He denies posting these—"

"Of course, he does. His denials are as ludicrous as your ridiculous assertion that these missiles are poorly drawn crayons."

I whispered to Maria, "I'm sorry. I tried my best." Did I? I wanted this finished before I got caught in the spiderweb.

The judge said, "Does the defendant wish to say anything before I pronounce her sentence? Young lady?"

Maria stood.

I reached for her hand. "Your Honor, she is only thirteen—"

"Old enough to know better," the judge snapped and glanced to the back of the room.

Maria pulled her hand free. "Daddy, you are my hero," she said and sat down.

Her words sealed her fate. There was nothing I could do for her.

"Defendant, stand," the judge ordered. "Your behavior was inspired by your father's treasonous actions." He stared at Maria. "Recognizing you are a child, easily led astray, trusting your father, I take pity on you. I am consigning you to an orphanage. I forbid any contact, personal or by any other means, with the criminal, whose name I shall not glorify in my court. As far as the law is concerned, you are no longer his child."

Maria trembled but held back tears.

I could not protest, as two matrons led Maria away without resistance. I felt like crying for the child and the country I love. I rose to beg the judge for mercy. His eyes were aimed at the doors.

Two men in dark suits stood silently in the back row. The taller man nodded grimly at Orlov. The other stared at me with a vulture's eye.

Judge Orlov had little choice. One child was a small sacrifice in the battle to control public opinion. Such a fuss over a child's drawing. The outside world was crying out for justice. Some would protest for a few days. And then? The indignation . . . memory will fade. That is the secret the rulers count on. Everything becomes old news. But I will not forget.

Several weeks later, I visited Maria in the orphanage. In a brown skirt and white buttoned blouse, she sat drawing quietly—a hawk-eyed matron nearby. The child did not smile when our eyes met. Her words were few. Emotionless. A short visit. Before I left, she handed me one of her many drawings. It was a child's crayoning: a little dog sitting among rabbits. All her drawings were of little smiling dogs and furry rabbits.

Note: This fictional story is meant as a tribute to the thirteen-year-old Russian, Maria Mosklyova, taken from her father after she drew a picture questioning Putin's Special Military Operation.

Where Time Stands Still

by Virginia Nygard

A dense and dark and eerie grove stands innocent in irony
for black oak and white ash fraternize
limbs entwined . . . embraced by pines
while spindly sumac braids its way between
—a scene less sinister than that below—

Bound in stoic silence they hover
where naked vines droop low and still
like exclamation points to show
—as if it could never happen now—
where lynch ropes
            hung
            long
            ago
    heavy with tormented flesh
    of   men
            women   and of
            children
            too
feared by impotent and frenzied folk
who deemed it the fitting thing to do

Stumps and boulders encompass this clandestine clearing
bright with blazing firelight   and
—like the sea's warning before a storm—
the air ripples with restless murmurs of those
come for the night's gathering

come awaiting the oxygen that will
fan to fire the sparks lurking within

Soon the steed of steel with eyes ablaze
rumbles near to the circle's rim
grumbles its discontent then halts in sullen silence
beside the others of its kind

A ghostly form arises from the steely glow
like a harlot bride gowned in unearned white
from hooded head to booted feet
with a blood-red slash across his chest
He strides to the circle's fire where those all dressed the same
    —too lame to show their cowardly faces—
stand assembled to plan evil for their fellow man

And the trees whisper on the breeze . . .

Still the addled roosters come to crow . . . and strut their plans for evil
deeds . . .
Powerless to turn our backs and go . . . again we watch them sow those
poison seeds . . .
We live where time stands still my friends . . . witnessing madness that
never ends

Life's Mysteries

by Mary Ellen Orvis

Can you tell me why the sun burns hot,
And why the sky's so blue,
why some people can tell only lies
and others can be true?

Can you explain why my dog goes lame,
why springtime flowers fade,
why nature can't simply turn aside
to save them from the fray?

I don't know when a sunset's swirls
will be the last I see,
or when the ocean's crashing waves
will cease their noisy spree.

I won't see if my mourners cry
or bless me with a prayer—
much as I'd love to see it all,
I simply won't be there.

Can you explain why lives come and go
like tides upon the beach,
to leave a mark, then fall away,
receding each in each?

Mission: Vanishing Act

by Janet K. Palmer

Archer knew what had to be done, but his secret mission would not be easy. It was an unusual one and went against the Guardian Angel Code of Ethics. They were not allowed to interfere unnecessarily in the lives of humans, but as he looked around the council table at his fellow guardian angels, each one nodded their assent. The vote was unanimous. No one beyond the Council knew what he was up to, but hopes were high for success, so he immediately took wing and headed for Earth.

When he arrived at Greta's school, he watched as she adjusted her backpack, tossed her freshly dyed red hair, took out her cell phone, and smiled at her own image. Taking a series of selfies, she checked the screen, chose the perfect one, and sent it off to her circle of anonymous admirers. Then she raced down the hall, barely making it to her last period history class before the bell rang.

Archer could tell Greta's mind was not on the history lesson. She kept trying to peek at her phone for responses to her latest upload. It was clear she was just biding her time before she could leave. When her quiz came back at the end of class with a *D* on it, she stuffed it into her backpack. Archer knew what she was thinking. *It's a passing grade; it will do.*

"No, young lady, it will not do," he muttered under his breath.

When Greta boarded the bus to head home, Archer hovered invisibly near the back. He noticed she wasn't the only one looking at her screen. Almost everyone on the bus was busily catching up on what they had missed during the day. The beautiful blue sky, spring blossoms, and swelling tree buds they passed along the way were totally lost on her. The only thing she seemed to notice was when the bus stopped and Ben's dog, spinning in circles of joy, greeted him as he got off. Archer could not read her thoughts, but he suspected she was wondering if adding a dog to her selfies would help boost her ratings. He sighed.

When she finally arrived home, Archer was already waiting for her. She couldn't see him, of course, but that was the whole point. For most of her thirteen years, he had secretly been nearby. She had kept him moderately busy with his keep-her-safe work, but lately he had run out of strategies to keep her safe, not from her usual bumps and bruises, but from her obsession with herself. His comrades were having similar problems with their teenage wards, which is why they finally put their heads together and came up with what might be a possible solution, Mission: Vanishing Act.

Greta was their first test subject.

Archer knew the trickiest part of the mission would be getting his hands on Greta's phone. She rarely let it out of her sight and even slept with it in case someone responded to one of her selfies.

It's no wonder she's tired all the time, he mused as he waited patiently for his opportunity to get his hands on her phone.

It came sooner than he expected. Amazingly, Greta deposited her backpack on the back of a kitchen chair, headed to the bathroom and, lo and behold, forgot to take her phone with her.

Archer quickly pulled out the phone, put the USB into the port, downloaded the experimental app they had devised, and slipped it back into her backpack just as Greta returned to the kitchen. With the program in place, now all he had to do was sit back and observe to see if it worked.

"What a pathetic snack stash," Greta said to no one in particular. Then, holding up a container of plain vanilla yogurt and sticking out her tongue, she turned her phone toward her face to take a selfie and saw . . . nothing.

Well, not entirely nothing. She could see the yogurt container, the kitchen all around her, and the clothes she was wearing, but her face, her hands, her whole physical self were nowhere on the screen. She tapped the screen to turn the lens. Everything in normal mode looked sharp, clear, and in focus. She tapped it back to selfie mode; she was still gone!

So far, so good. Archer laughed silently. *I wonder what she'll do next? It will be fun to see if each reaction follows the algorithm precisely.*

Greta's mother arrived home from work a few minutes later to find Greta in a frantic tizzy. After calming her daughter down enough to find out what the problem was, she took Greta's phone to check it out for herself.

"It seems to be working just fine for me, honey," her mother said. "Look, I even took a selfie, and there I am. Here, let me try to take one of the two of us together."

Pulling her reluctant daughter next to her, she snapped a selfie of the two of them and then showed Greta the photo she had taken. There they were, crystal clear—her mother with the indulgent face she tried to maintain at all costs and Greta looking terrified.

Archer consulted his notes. *Yes! Things are going exactly as planned.*

Storming off to her room, Archer began checking off one box after another as Greta frantically tried to fix her phone. Restart it, *check.* Take one picture after another, *check.* Take a picture of herself in the mirror with no success, *check.* Repeat each step again and again, *check.* Finally, she gave up, exhausted, and decided to do her homework. Archer checked off the last box.

And that will be it for today.

On the bus the next morning, most of the kids were still absorbed in their phones, but Archer could tell Greta was noticing her surroundings for the first time in ages. She had no desire to talk to her bus mates though, especially about selfless selfies. She finally perked up as Ben boarded the bus. His dog was straining at the leash, trying to follow him, as his mother waved and continued on her walk with the dog in tow.

Greta finally spoke.

"What kind of dog is that?" she asked as she motioned for Ben to sit in the empty seat next to her.

———

Archer was the guest of honor when The Council of Guardian Angels reconvened six weeks later. They all listened intently to his report on the new app. Greta's fear of others thinking she was going crazy had prevented her from discussing her "broken" phone with anyone else. They all agreed. The new app was genius!

Archer pulled out his tablet to show them the latest pictures Greta had taken: ones of her new dog, some nature shots, and a few of herself with family and friends.

Archer's job was done, but there was still work to do. The order was given for full implementation, and a host of guardian angels winged their way toward Earth.

The Extravagant Infatuation

by Pamela Peffer

C hloe Masters sliced open the last and largest storage box with her utility knife as her friend Meghan Wild hung a painting in the only open wall space in Chloe's Brooklyn apartment.

"Chloe, where in the name of sanity are you going to hang that painting? We've covered every inch of wall from floor to ceiling. This apartment looks like an art gallery. Stop already."

"There's space above my bed for this one." Chloe carved through the butcher paper and tore it off.

An awkward silence filled the room as the two women eyed the last piece of art, mouths agape and hands on hips, shock coloring both their faces. Meghan pierced their prolonged silence with a thought-provoking, "Suitable for hanging over your bed?"

Chloe wrinkled her nose. "Maybe not."

"Who's the artist, and who's the babe?"

Chloe squatted to read the signature. "R. Cassuoli. Never heard of him. Have you?"

"You're asking me? Chloe, my art gallery of choice is Walmart."

Chloe chuckled, crossed her arms, and paced back and forth before the portrait of the naked woman. She broke her gaze and walked to her bookshelf filled with photo albums. Thumbing through the album labeled 1966, she removed one photo and returned, comparing the photographic image to the face of the woman in the painting.

"She's my grandmother."

Meghan stared at the photograph in Chloe's hand. "This is certainly an *oh-là-là* moment. Doctor Cindy was hot stuff. Do you think they were lovers?"

Chloe smacked Meghan's arm. "Shut up."

"I'm not judging her. She was maybe twenty-three? Not married to Doctor David? How romantic to pose nude for an artist—maybe a lover—while he paints your portrait. Wonder what happened to him?"

"I don't know. I've never seen this painting."

"I wonder why?"

"Meghan, please," Chloe scoffed, twisting a lock of her hair. "I'm trying to process your idea. An Italian lover?" She kneeled down and slid her hands across the frame and dust cover. "What are these lumps?" With her knife, she carved away the dust cover, revealing two bulging manila envelopes resting in the lower corners of the frame. "Envelopes?"

"Secret treasure? Open them up."

Chloe tore back the flap of one envelope and peered inside. "Jewelry," she said, as she dumped the contents, and a tangled assortment of watches, necklaces, rings, bracelets, and earrings clinked against the hardwood floor. "How odd."

From the second envelope, she pulled out a handful of paper items. "Letters . . . from R. Cassuoli and photos." She paged through the letters while Meghan sifted through the photographs. "Postmarks are Rome and New York City, dated 1966 and 1967." She opened one of the letters. "It's written in Italian. He closes with '*Ti amo*, Romano.'"

"It means 'I love you.'" Meghan fanned out several photos. "Look, have you ever seen such a beautiful man?"

"Never. Sue Tancreto speaks Italian. I'll ask her to translate these."

"Good idea."

———

Sue sat cross-legged on Chloe's couch, savoring the taste of her coffee as she finished reading the last letter.

"Did Doctor Cindy give you these?"

"They were inside the framing of a painting she bequeathed to me."

"Interesting storage place. Chloe, I'll give you a summary translation, not a word-for-word read."

"Why is that?"

"You said Doctor Cindy and Doctor David were married in 1970?"

"Yes, late 1970."

"Good to know. She knew this Romano Cassuoli prior to that time. Chloe, these letters are a little steamy. In fact, R-rated."

"Oh . . . okay. Just an executive summary, then."

"Wise choice. They met in Rome in 1966. He was a flight attendant for Alitalia Airlines and an aspiring artist, she a medical student at Columbia University." She pointed to the logo embossed on some of the stationery. "In 1967, his home base became New York City where she lived, yet he continued to send her love letters. Perhaps because she was busy with med school, they couldn't meet often. He asked her to share an apartment, but she declined, pleading the rigors of her studies.

"Something caused a rift between them. He said he kept the jewelry for them, and it would provide an investment for their future. He told her to keep it safe. And that was the last letter."

"I'm curious why she kept these letters."

"No clue. I wish you had her last letter to him. It might reveal how their story ended."

"Well, thanks, Sue. You've helped a lot. By the way, I found that he's alive and living here in New York City."

"And you won't rest until you find him and unravel the story of their romance?"

"Correct."

———

Chloe paced the sidewalk in front of the Museum of the City of New York, their agreed rendezvous location.

"Chloe."

Her heart leapt as a male voice called out behind her. She turned to find him walking toward her, posture erect, silver hair slicked back, olive skin tanned by the sun, and brown eyes like lasers piercing through her. He was handsome enough to pose for the cover of GQ for seniors, if such an edition existed.

"Romano?"

He took her hand and kissed her fingers. "You resemble Cindy. Come, there's a café inside. Let's enjoy a coffee."

They walked up the grand staircase to the second-floor café. She found a table by the window; he ordered coffee and returned, placing a cup before her. "Heavy cream, no sugar."

"How did you guess?"

"Cindy drank her coffee that way."

Chloe circled the rim of her cup with her finger. "Grandma introduced me to coffee. You remember how she took hers after fifty years?"

"I remember so many things about her, many I'd not dare comment on."

Chloe lowered her eyes to her cup as heat rose in her cheeks. "Please stop."

"I apologize. I've made you feel uncomfortable." He folded his hands and lowered his gaze as well. "Your grandmother had a good life?"

"From my vantage point, she had the best life and gave her bountiful life gifts to so many." Chloe reached inside her oversized shoulder bag, pulled out a fat manila envelope, and slid it across the table. "I came here to give you these."

"Photographs?" He peered inside the envelope and furrowed his brow.

"No, spoils of your air-travel career. Items passengers lost that you should have sent to lost and found."

"You think I stole these items?"

"I know you did. Your letters reveal your crime."

Tension crackled between them. "She was a once-in-a-lifetime love I couldn't afford. I was completely infatuated."

"So, you became a common thief to impress her? You made her an accessory after the fact. She could have gone to jail. She hid the jewelry inside the framing of her nude portrait."

"She was beautiful and clever."

Chloe drummed her fingers on the table. "No regrets, Romano? The statute of limitations has expired on this crime. You're off the hook."

He slid the envelope back her way. "Sell it, Chloe. Buy yourself a hot car."

"Tempting me to embrace your ethics?"

His sly grin spoke volumes.

She reached for the envelope. "I'll sell it and donate the proceeds in your name to Grandma's pediatric care foundation."

Romano smiled and nodded. "She'd appreciate that."

Secret

by Paula Pivko

something that is kept or meant to be kept unknown or <u>unseen</u> by others.

A secret is a thing of stone.
It sits within the soul.
And no one wants it to sing
because it could hurt us all.

It is born of pain,
hummingbird size.
On its body is
written in blood,
words unspoken, and
from them nothing to gain.
Or is there?

I hate you.
I love you.
I wish you'd never been born.
I'm sorry you never were.

Keep it caged, bear the weight.
Because if it ever escaped
It might grow wings and
Destroy those you love.

I have stolen
I have cheated.

I am not who
You think I am.

Its beak is sharp as truth.
So clip its wings and keep
It caged. For it could
Tear the veil and illusion
Others see about you.
Or they could take it
for power and
for pleasure.
Even the threat is enough
to hide it away.

But a secret imprisons.
That is what people say.
Share it to be set free.
Or break another's heart.
Pick well who you gift it to.
Lest they let it go and it
Ruins those you love.
Pick well who sees
lest they know you for what
you truly are.

Martha and Jerry

by William R. Platt

I throw open the shade and the gray light of a snowy afternoon floods our bedroom. Outside our window, a fine white powder covers the bare branches of our front-yard maple tree.

"Wake up, sleepyhead." I try to keep my tone cheerful as I throw back the shades on the second window. "How are you feeling?"

Martha, my wife, blinks through her drowsiness, tries to rise to elbows, and leans against the headboard.

"Oooh, that hurt." She grimaces and slumps back into the bed.

"Let me help."

I sit beside her, fluff the pillows, and help to prop her up.

"How's that? Comfy?"

"This damn disease is taking over my whole body, Jerry. Everything hurts."

"I brought you something that will help." On the nightstand there is a warm bowl of soup and the ever-present glass of ice water with a straw. "Here, try some of this." I coax a spoonful of broth between her lips. She smiles with appreciation.

"Mmm, chicken noodle, my favorite."

"Yes, I know."

"Really? I thought it was a secret."

"Sweetheart, we've been married for forty years. There are very few secrets left between us, and chicken soup ain't one of them."

I dab a spot of soup from her lower lip and offer a sip of water. Her blue eyes still sparkle, and her smile is as warm as sunshine, but the disease is taking a toll. The circles under her eyes are dark, and her hair is growing back thin and gray.

"It's quiet," she says. "I can't hear the kids. Have they finished opening their presents?"

"Christmas was yesterday, sweetheart. Rob has to work tomorrow. They left this morning to go back home. Debbie and the kids wanted to come upstairs and say goodbye, but I thought it best to let you sleep."

I see the disappointment painted across her face.

"Well, at least I got to see her one last time before—"

"Stop that," I cut her short. "You'll see them all again."

My abruptness catches her off guard. I feed her another spoonful. It's too much, and she begins to cough. I use a napkin to catch the flecks of soup and blood. She takes a drink of water and sinks deeper into the pillow as the coughing abates. She looks tired and resigned but, somehow, not defeated.

"We've had a good life. Haven't we, Jerry?" she asks.

I lower the tray to the floor and pause for a moment before placing my hand on hers.

"Yes, of course, sweetheart, we've had a wonderful life. There's been a few rough patches, but we always got through them."

"I don't think we're going to get through this patch, sweetie."

"We might. I got a few secrets up my sleeve."

"You're a computer programmer at the university. Do you have a program to cure breast cancer?"

"No, I don't have a cure for cancer, but technology might be able to provide alternative solutions."

"Like what?"

"That's a secret I'm keeping to myself."

Martha scans my features, looking for a hint into my thoughts. She makes a decision, and I know I'm not getting the last word.

"You can't solve every problem with technology, Jerry."

"Computers are getting smarter every day. Who knows, maybe one will find a cure."

"It better hurry. My time is getting short. And if there is no cure, you better get used to life without me."

"I know, sweetheart. You've taught me how to deal with all the surprises life throws at us and how we have to accept the good and the bad things that happen to us."

"That's right. Sometimes the best surprises come from the worst circumstances. Like Debbie's car accident? We thought she would never walk again. But along came Rob, the perfect physical therapist, and now the two of them have been married for ten years, and they have two beautiful children."

"Beautiful children? Those kids are earth-shattering troublemakers, just like their mother. Only difference is there are two of them, which makes them double the trouble."

"Debbie is a wonderful daughter," she says, "and an even better mother."

"Yes, Debbie's awesome. And she's a great musician, just like you. I wouldn't change anything about her. But what about us? What would you change?"

"Well, there is the glaring matter of your botched marriage proposal. Most girls don't dream of being proposed to in a bowling alley between the seventh and eighth frames."

"And here I thought putting the engagement ring in your glass of beer was the height of romance."

"I almost choked on it."

"Okay, I'll do better next time."

She closes her eyes and squeezes my hand. "A little late for that, don't you think?"

"Not if I remember."

"You never remember anything."

"I remember the important things, like the day we met. I was walking through Overland Park on my way home when I heard music coming from the meadow. I made my way up the hill, and there you were, sitting among the wildflowers practicing your flute."

She smiles at the memory. "Impressive. Do you remember the song I was playing?"

"'Greensleeves,' and you were terrible."

"Excuse me? I'll have you know I sat in the first chair of the Riverside High School Orchestra."

"Yes, sweetheart, you were the best."

Her eyes are closed, and she's breathing evenly. I think she's asleep, smiling at her dreams.

I find the smart phone in my shirt pocket, activate the screen, and check the settings. Everything is ready, except for the final adjustments.

"What's that?" Martha is awake, eager to see what I'm doing.

"No, no. This is my secret. It's a surprise."

The phone is connected to a hidden program running in the background on the server at the university. Under the settings tab, I find the options for character traits. For Martha, I select FORGET, and for me, I choose to REMEMBER. Then, I hit RESTART.

The snow in the front yard stops falling. For a moment everything is as still as a portrait. Then the maple tree dissolves into electronic bytes that tumble into nothingness. The windows and walls of our bedroom shimmer and disappear. Tables, chairs, rug, and floor follow until only Martha and I remain, floating on an endless gray cloud. I touch PAUSE.

Her beautiful smile and twinkling eyes are locked in place. Her expression is bemused with excitement. I've surprised her again.

I place my lips against hers. I taste and feel her warmth. In that kiss, that instant of electronic interaction, there is love. I pull away, wondering what I would ever do without her.

"Don't worry, sweetheart. We'll have more surprises."

I touch the controls on the phone, and she is gone. I am gone. Everything is gone.

MSDOS: INITIATE: SAVED_PROGRAM: MARTHA/ JERRY_1988_RESET_#3

INSTALL_UPDATES: YES_/_2036

A moment later, I'm walking through Overland Park taking the shortcut home after school. Up the hill, past the trees, there's a meadow where the wildflowers are blooming. A young flutist with twinkling blue eyes and a dazzling smile is struggling with "Greensleeves."

Hiding Beneath

by Stefanie Posteraro

The water is quiet.
Mangroves cast shadows and shimmer.
Night fishermen troll for bait.
Skillfully spreading glow-in-the-dark nets with a soft splat—
sinking silently into the black.
This conversation's open while we glide.
Above the dark.
Occasionally the water's fish swish,
Asserting their presence.
Beckoning us beneath.
To their dark and wild world of slimy, handless creatures—eating,
struggling and dying.
Hiding in dark kelp weeds to stakeout prey.
Leaving coral restaurants well fed.
The conch protects his fleshy blob by being recluse and grouchy.
The jellyfish—untouchable, arrogant and free-spirited.
Expands, contracts, and carelessly drags
her pretty tendrils of poison.
They dare us to touch.
We are bigger, smarter and have opposing thumbs.
But down below, they know
we'll never survive without clunk.
They gaze up at us skeptical,
giving us their side eye—and half smiles.
Amused and bemused by us,
and what we hide beneath.

Wine and Words

by Barbara Rein

The Adirondack chair sat a stunning ten feet high on the front lawn of the Sonoma, California winery. Taller still was my daughter's list of mistakes I'd made in her upbringing. This trip from New York to explain my temporary separation from her father brought out a torrent of hurts she'd been holding inside for years— pain I never knew she carried. Everything, it seems, was my fault.

Real or imagined, it didn't matter. Her perception was her reality. Daddy's little girl didn't want to hear my side of the marital problems. Nor did she want to hear the whys of my deportment from years ago. Her side was the only side—the important one.

As we roamed the winery estate, words emerged between tasting room sips. Feelings, slights, and affronts that should have been aired when she was a teen, poured from her like spilled Chardonnay. If I made notice of her lovely, blond curls, she saw it as my putting emphasis on her looks. My comments about her brother's exceptional grades were taken as demeaning to her own. She berated me for keeping her from going out in high school. Yet it was she who withdrew from friends and activities after a severe case of chicken pox left her with facial scars. No amount of coaxing could get her out of her depression then. And the reality of that time could not be voiced now. Her focus, her anguish, radiated from a singular view.

Like a bitter, tannin-filled Syrah, all this and more I swallowed. For two hours she chastised me. For two hours I apologized. And she began to hear my sincerity. When we strolled to the front lawn of the winery, the Adirondack chair seemed the last hurdle to climb. Hand over foot, we made it to the seat, two women with an enormous problem that, sitting close together, now seemed as small as we looked on that giant chair. Further out on the lawn, a massive, empty picture frame hung between two poles planted in the ground. The ornate frame captured a vista of drab, cloud-streaked sky. My daughter took my hand, her fingers lacing into mine. Though the sun remained hidden, a brilliance blurred my eyes. With secrets unbound, I saw not an approaching storm, but an open, honest future with my daughter. It's a picture that hangs in my heart still.

The One and Only

by Allan K. Roit

Professor Roberts was the most popular teacher at my college. His breadth of knowledge and ability to convey it in simple, understandable language brought students from various departments to his classes. Younger than most senior professors, he was tall, thin, had a dark complexion and dark hair, with an open, smiling face, and slight accent I couldn't place.

As a freshman, I attended his Introduction to Western Civilization class—one of those large intro classes held in an auditorium. The professor wore a lavalier mic, walked the aisles, and never stood at the lectern. He was required to use the slides provided for the class but rarely read them. His lectures veered off from standard rote history to aspects of art, architecture, economics, philosophy, and science. He would always say, "What good is the study of history without understanding that events inherently contain the culture of the time in which they occurred? These function as catalysts for the future."

Each year, I took one or two of his classes. During my junior year, he asked if I would be his TA, teaching assistant. We ended up working together through the end of my senior year. Occasionally, he asked that I come to his house to help him with research projects. The first time I visited him, I stood in awe at the large Victorian mansion on the outskirts of town. I thought, *This is not a teacher's house, but speaks of old money. He must have inherited it.*

An entrance hall and staircase led to side hallways with rooms on either side. Wood everywhere—from the wainscoted walls, stairs, floors, ceiling, and doors. He called the first room on the right his "working" library. It contained a large, wooden partner's desk with chairs on either side and one large, leather chair. Bookcases covered the walls with reference volumes and valuable collectibles. Three other libraries stood along the two corridors. Professor Roberts kept one of the rear libraries locked. It contained his most valuable items, and he apologetically said, "I hope you won't take offense; it's just one of my idiosyncratic quirks."

During my senior year, I prepared submission packages for various graduate programs in history. The professor supportively drafted a glowing recommendation letter, signed, as usual, by *H.G. Roberts*. I always wondered what the H.G. stood for, but, when asked, he shrugged, "Just an old family name that I never really liked."

As the school year wound to its end, our current work schedule and activities grew three-fold. The professor had a book due for completion; I had tests and final papers to write and, as TA, to grade. We worked opposite each other on that large partner's desk in the working library.

One day, the professor asked me to "hold down the fort" while he went to the post office.

Tired more than usual, I nodded off.

The fire alarm jolted me awake. Running for the door, I paused— *The books; how could I leave them?* My thoughts turned to the rear library with all its valuable contents. Turning, I ran down the corridor. There was no smoke evident. The library door was locked. I shoved it with my shoulder until the jamb shattered.

Inside, it was dark and dusty. Still no sign of a fire. I raised the shade of the one window and prepared to toss things out onto the lawn. There was no desk and only one large, comfortable chair. Large, glass bookcases covered three walls. The fourth wall held framed documents and diplomas. Obviously, these objects had sentimental value, so I got those first. I reached for an Old English certificate of some sort and recognized what looked like the name "Hieronymus Gilgamesh Roberts." Some ancestor did him a disservice. No wonder he hated his name.

Grabbing more frames without reading them, I saw a large handwritten certificate entitled, "*Universitates Scholarium Bologna.*" Below some Latin script was a series of signatures including a distinctive *H.R. Rüber*. Blurred with age, the handwriting was as familiar to me as my own.

Shaking my head, I continued to gather frames, easing them out the window. When I was done, I turned to the glass case on the other side of the room. The lower level contained cubby holes with rolled up parchments and a large area housing stones with etched hieroglyphics. It was while looking at these objects that I noticed the alarm had gone off, and standing in the doorway was Professor Roberts.

"I'm sorry you had to go through all this trouble," he said. "It was just a short in the alarm system, but I appreciate you caring enough to save things I hold precious."

Pointing at the now empty wall, I said, "Who are you?"

Wearily sitting on the one chair in the room, he pointed around us. "This is my life. I've been known by many names over the years. My earliest memories are from Mesopotamia, hence the name Gilgamesh, after the hero carved on that stone next to you."

With no other chair in the room, I slumped to the ground, waiting for more.

"Every century or so, I've come to expect that someone would discover my secret. If you search records carefully, there are references to me—fictions of a Methuselah who lived through the ages. You may even write such a story yourself someday. I have been very lucky to find people willing to keep my secret."

Rising from his seat, he held out a hand and helped me up. I had so many questions but said nothing as he led me to the front door.

"It has been a pleasure working with you," he said.

Walking down the front steps, I turned and said, "Your secret is safe with me."

He smiled and said, "I know."

Some weeks later, I returned to the house. A woman came down the steps. She was a real estate agent and allowed me to look around. There were no books anywhere, just bare shelves. On my way out, she asked me to sign a guest book. When she saw my name, she said, "Wait, I've been expecting you. The previous owner left a package with your name on it."

Inside the package, I found the certificate from Bologna. After many subsequent weeks of research, I discovered it was from the first university of Europe, signed by their first graduating class: a guild of learned men whose idea it was to create an institution of higher learning.

Today, I am a university professor myself, having received my PhD with a ground-breaking dissertation on the growth of European universities. For many years, people in our community wondered what happened to H.G. Roberts. I think of him often.

Soon, I will have to move on myself. What constantly amazes me is how learned men do not always see the nose in front of their faces. How could Professor Roberts be so smart after living so many years and still think he was the only one?

You see, I *can* keep a secret.

Marriage Secrets #3

by E.A. Russo

Olivia lounges with legs outstretched on their L-shaped sofa, pretending to read her Kindle but unable to focus. Chicago lights twinkle a dark cityscape beyond the floor-to-ceiling windows of their one-bedroom apartment. It's nearly nine. Any minute now, her husband will take Peanut, their corgi, out one final time before bed.

From the bedroom, the only place to get away with everyone home, David fields a work emergency with his signature calm. "Send over what you've got, and I'll work on it tonight . . ."

She watches the crack of the bedroom door and taps her screen to turn the page, only so her device won't go to sleep. Her husband of twenty-four years wanders in and out of sight as he speaks into his earbuds. "We can't reschedule. It's tomorrow morning."

At her feet, Peanut stretches, yawns, and hops down from the sofa. She bounces on her front feet at the door, yapping twice.

It's time.

"I gotta go," David says. "Send me what you have, and I'll take a look. Yep, see you tomorrow."

Peanut lets out a more insistent bark. The bedroom door opens, and David comes out, running a hand through his chestnut hair. He looks tired but smiles warmly at Olivia.

"Do you need me to take her out?" she asks. *Please say no.* All her energy goes into appearing nonchalant.

"No, I could use the fresh air." He clips the leash onto Peanut's harness, and the dog lurches toward the front door. "I'll be back in about an hour."

As the door closes behind him, she grips her Kindle and waits.

The elevator dings in the hallway, and she imagines them getting in. She sets a forty-minute timer on her phone, a safe buffer before they return.

Olivia transfers herself to the wheelchair waiting for her at the edge of the sofa. The Chair, as she calls it, was supposed to be temporary until she recovered, but that day keeps slipping farther and farther away.

Quickly navigating to the bedroom, she opens the closet and pulls at a blanket draped just so in the back, exposing a rectangular instrument case.

A familiar wave of cold nausea washes over her, making her pause, but her violin calls to her. In her head, a sonata plays. The song is stuck there, haunting her. Leaning forward, she drags the case out of the closet and onto the made bed. She unzips the cover, pinches the clasp, and draws the top open. The bitter smell of rosin greets her.

Gleaming amber wood that always felt so alive and full of potential now brings painful memories of the last few practice sessions. How foreign the instrument felt in her hands. How damage to her shoulder limited her bow stroke. How her fingers fumbled across the strings. Her instrument's betrayal hurt worse than any procedure during these past ten months.

Without her violin, Olivia doesn't know who she is.

One unlucky moment, forty-three weeks of surgeries and recovery, and now nothing would ever be the same. Things that gave her joy don't make her feel good at all anymore. But she couldn't imagine life without music. She couldn't give up. Not yet.

With a delicate touch, Olivia runs a finger along the smooth varnish, even though she knows the oils from her hands are bad for the finish.

Only a few scales, she tells herself, tightening the bow, *before David gets back*. She hates keeping things from him, but if he knew Olivia was trying to play again, he'd have such hope. He'd been the best support through all this, but she couldn't bear to dash his optimism—that might break them both.

She tunes up and plays a hesitant G-major scale, more scales, and her go-to warmup.

Notes reverberate against the bedroom walls, and the cotton duvet dampens the sound. Bedroom acoustics don't compare to her old practice room, but at least the notes are clear.

Now for the piece she was supposed to play when her world fell apart. The one she can't let go, not until she hears it again in full.

Slow and soft, she starts. As her fingers find their way, she forcibly clears her mind, letting muscle memory take over. Note after note, she approaches the song's bridge, where she stumbled last time. This time she closes her eyes and hopes the notes are there.

D avid returns from their walk but doesn't enter the apartment. Instead, he sits cross-legged outside their door, Peanut at his side, listening.

As Olivia approaches the bridge, where she struggled last time, he signals Peanut to stay quiet. He dreads the missed notes and the anguished sobs that follow these stolen practices. It kills him not to run to his wife and comfort her, but he knows instinctively this struggle is personal. David can't play the notes for her. He needs Olivia to remember how to fight again.

One distracted driver, a single text, meant the difference between his bubbly wife walking to an audition to secure her seat in the philharmonic and this new life of hospitals, surgeries, and pain.

He wished he could somehow undo everything, take them back to before, when her eyes glowed with passion instead of darkening in defeat.

Three weeks ago, he'd returned early and discovered these unsteady notes. She hid her playing from him. Initially, her secret stung, but now he understands.

Recovery is more than physical. Olivia's faith in herself has been so tenuous lately, he couldn't risk saying anything. That she is playing at all means she hasn't given up.

Now she approaches the song's bridge, and he holds his breath.

With each note she lands, the tone of her music turns confident. Up and over the tricky part, she plays at full volume. He clenches his fist in victory. Her usual flourish isn't there, but this was progress.

The last chord fades, and she begins again. Halfway through a third time, an alarm trills, and the music stops.

Peanut sits up. David puts a finger to his lips, quietly gets to his feet, and they slip out through the stairwell to the floor below. They ride the elevator to the lobby, waste ten minutes, and return.

Now Olivia's back on the sofa, as if she never moved. But her Kindle's upside down, and there's a new sparkle in her obsidian eyes.

He lets Peanut loose. "I gotta go back to the office to fix some numbers." He grabs his laptop case and kisses her, running a hand through her sleek, dark hair. "See you in the morning."

"I was about to go to bed anyway," she says, with an unconvincing yawn. "You can work here."

David ignores her and kisses her again. Olivia needs more practice time, and that is one thing he *can* do for her. "It's okay. I'll get more done at the office."

He closes the door with a solid click. Seconds later, The Chair creaks. A moment passes, and the melody again drifts from their apartment before the elevator even arrives.

David slumps against the wall with an exhale. *Thank, God.* She could never know how close he was to losing hope, too.

French Lessons

by Ruth Senftleber

In my senior year of high school, French brought me anguish and joy. As the principal's daughter, I pressured myself to be the best in everything. My father had a whole high school to worry about, and my mother kept telling me to relax, but I was locked into over-achiever mode. No doubt I was overcompensating for my above-average height, awful red hair, and lack of a boyfriend.

One October Tuesday, I was in the school newspaper office, a tiny room off the main office, typing an article for the next edition. A knock at the open door interrupted my thoughts. Jean-Paul Garnier stood there, smiling. Our French exchange student was my best friend Lindsay's boyfriend.

"I theenk you like a French *perspective* for your *journal*, *oui?*" He held out a rigid floppy disk. "Cleeck on first file."

I inserted the disk into the computer and clicked, my heart racing. We were in AP French together, so I'd had time to observe him up close. He was dark-haired, handsome, and very French, and I loved how he said his last name, *Garn-yea*.

I scanned the article, impressed by his comparison of school here with that in his native France. I could fix his grammar and typos.

"Sure, I'll publish your piece. Thanks." I copied and pasted it, ejected the disk, and handed it back. His hand brushed mine, and I could feel my face flush.

"Is okay to say your hair is beautiful, yes?" His brown eyes looked into my green ones. "Even if you are best friend of Lindsay?"

"Uh, I guess so." No one except my parents ever called my curly, red hair beautiful. "*Merci*" was all I could say, and he left with a puzzled look on his face. I kicked myself over my ineptness. Lindsay would have said something adorable.

Two weeks later, Jean-Paul brought me another article, this one about life as an exchange student. He dropped into the spare chair beside the computer desk, and we chatted in French and English. I could almost forget he was Lindsay's boyfriend. This was newspaper business, after all.

In the following months, Jean-Paul brought me other stories about life in France. I looked forward to our chats more than to his articles. We discovered we loved music, especially Vivaldi and Def Leppard, and disliked American football. Like me, he had a younger sister, and he was homesick for his family in Paris. I told him about life as the principal's daughter. We talked about almost everything.

I never told Lindsay about those Tuesdays.

In early May, the prom committee announced its theme: An Evening in Paris. I started the article about it, wanting to finish quickly so I wouldn't think about being dateless for my senior prom. My dad would dance with me, and I would watch Lindsay and Jean-Paul having a wonderful time. It would be heartbreaking.

A knock on the office doorframe startled me, and I looked up to see Jean-Paul put his finger to his lips. He produced a red rose from behind his back and held it out to me with a flourish, as he dropped to one knee. I took it, stabbing a thorn into my thumb. No one had ever given me a rose.

"*Ma chérie* Gail, would you do me the honor of going to the prom with me?" He took my hand and kissed it, just like in the movies. I felt light-headed. Then Lindsay's face floated through my mind.

"I can't go with you. Lindsay's my best friend." My eyes filled with tears. My long friendship with Lindsay had taken a back seat during the year, as she spent most of her free time with Jean-Paul. When we talked on the phone, the conversation was always about him. I didn't want to hurt her.

"*Non*. I—how do you say? —break up with her a week ago." He regained his feet. "All of you are very kind to me. But most of all, you make me feel *chez moi*—at home—here." He gestured around the small office. "I could not continue with Lindsay. Did she not tell you?"

"No, but I can't do that to her." Sweat beaded up on my forehead. I laid the rose on the desk, saved and closed the prom file, and shut down the computer. "I need to leave." I grabbed my books and purse and brushed past him, ignoring his hurt look.

"*Alors*, I will not go to your prom," he called after me.

I sobbed all the way to my car. I had never had a serious boyfriend, and now I had Lindsay's. What had I done? I could never tell her about his invitation.

In the three weeks before prom, Lindsay called every night, agonizing over the break-up. She had waited to tell me, sure he would change his mind, and now I couldn't tell her she was hoping in vain.

Prom and graduation passed in a blur. True to his word, Jean-Paul did not appear at the dance. Lindsay arrived with a football player, and I served punch. Heartbreaking indeed.

As valedictorian, I sat on the graduation stage with the administrators, faculty, and class officers. Midway through the program, Jean-Paul spoke about his year as an exchange student. When he finished, he thanked those on the stage for their support, looking straight at me for several moments.

Afterwards, Lindsay grabbed my arm. "That long look Jean-Paul gave you." Her voice rose. "What was that about?"

"He was thanking everyone, my dad, the teachers—"

"And you! What's going on?"

"Nothing. Really." I shivered under my gown. I'd given up an opportunity for her but could say nothing.

Now I'm picking up my name badge at our thirtieth reunion, the first one I've attended. I step out of the way to pin it on and scan the incoming crowd, searching faces for their eighteen-year-old selves. Then I spot her.

Lindsay at forty-eight, in a royal-blue suit, a few gray strands in her impeccably styled hair, is still stunning. She's twenty or thirty pounds heavier, but she carries them well. She gets her badge from the table and turns, and I take a deep breath. The moment of truth has arrived.

She sees me, comes over, and enfolds me in a hug. As she steps back, her eyebrows rise as she notices my badge.

"Gail Allen Garnier." She smiles. "I knew you worked for a publishing company in New York after college. I didn't know you got married."

I shrug. "I joined their Paris branch." *Time to confess*, I think. "And renewed an acquaintance."

She stares. "Jean-Paul? You found him in France?" Her face looks surprised, not suspicious. "The internet finds lost people, right?"

I choose not to say that I never lost him, that he wrote me a long letter, apologizing for coming between friends and asking for a second chance. We kept in touch throughout college, our early jobs, and other relationships. When I moved to Paris, we dated and then married. Our boys are teenagers; both have my red hair, which pleases Jean-Paul.

Some secrets are best kept, after all.

Proteus Ascending #7

by H.G. Silvia

The howling wind of this alien world whistles over the fuselage. Methane ice crystals crash against its skin. I close my eyes and see memories of hail storms in New Orleans, the hot tin roof protecting Josh and me.

Josh. My twin.

A feeling of . . . loss.

A button blinks on a console, urging me to press it. A recorded message plays.

"Mother, this is Ares-1, Mission Specialist Daphne Stearns. At 0800 hours, Commander Willoughby and S.O. Trask suited up and attempted a landing site survey. Severe weather rolled in, causing zero visibility. Soon after, we lost comms due to interference from aerosolized copper within the storm. This would have made their suits' acoustical triangulators unreliable. I enabled the lander's visual beacon, hoping they would find their way back. That was nearly sixteen hours ago. Despite the ongoing storm, I am going out to search for them."

I am Daphne Stearns. I cannot fly this lander.

Fear.

Hunger overwhelms me. I rip open a ration pack and choke down the soy-based slurry. The screen displays -200°C outside. Copper-methane ice covers the ship. I keep the airlock temps above freezing for Willoughby. If he doesn't make it, I don't make it. I need a pilot.

Willoughby is the pilot. I remain imprisoned here without him. I want to be Willoughby.

Desire.

Will I make it back to Earth or live the rest of my miserable, short life on this icy prison planet? Maybe the storm will pass, and comms will return. Maybe Josh was right. Maybe I shouldn't have run to space to get away from Dad. Maybe Josh would have understood if I told him what Dad did. Too late.

Shame.

My mind is a chaotic mess of memories and emotions. I hate it.

Hate.

That's new, too. No, I hated Dad. Focus.

A Klaxon howls from the aft. I rush to the airlock and peer out the thick-polymer window. Willoughby waves his forearm, alight with digital brilliance, back and forth past the porthole. The interior and exterior lights fire up, and the airlock sequence begins.

He's alone. Having Trask's O_2 explains how he survived this long. The light turns orange, and he stumbles inside. Off comes his EVA suit, and despite the freezing temps outside, his jumper is soaked through with sweat. UV light douses him, and in an instant, he's cleared to come inside the lander.

He sucks up fresh oxygen in exhausted gulps and climbs into his pilot seat. He looks at me as if he's seen a ghost.

"Strap in. We're buggin' out."

"What about Trask?" I already know the answer.

Dark eyes in an ashen face dart left to right before settling squarely on me. A deep breath and a hard swallow precede his news. "We were attacked."

"Attacked? By what? When?" Again, I know the answer.

"When the storm started, Trask and I linked up a safety line, and we headed back here." While he speaks, he flips switches, and punches commands into the flight computer.

Hope.

I won't be trapped on this rock. I won't die here. I fight the urge to smile. "What attacked you?"

He shakes his head again. "It was too fast. Never saw it. Never heard it. One second, I felt the tension of Trask on the line. The next, it went slack. I heard him scream. I turned, and he was gone."

I remember probes finding no indigenous life on this planet. "Did you pursue it?"

His face becomes a grimace, and those dark eyes release tears. "I followed bloody drag marks in the snow, maybe twenty yards, before finding him. Parts of him, anyway."

Trask is dead. Be human. Comfort him. I reach out for Willoughby's hand.

"Jesus, you're ice cold." He recoils and rubs the spot I touched.

I buckle into the co-pilot's seat. Trask's seat. I offer an excuse. "I tried to conserve power to give you more time to make it back."

He nods. "After hours of walking blind, I found a cliff. There was an artificial light visible below. I could have sworn it was your personal beacon flashing in the fog. I assumed you came out for us and fell over." He scanned me again, seeing I was not lying in a foggy open grave, and returned to comms. "Mother, this is Ares-1. Preparing for emergency dust-off of LZ. ETA to rendezvous fifteen mikes, over."

He doesn't know about the comms yet.

The radio returns only white noise. This evokes memories of a trip to the ocean. St. Augustine, summer between seventh and eighth grade. Josh and I slept on the beach. He was afraid of sand fleas and whined all night. He was right. We woke up damp, covered in bites.

Regret.

The propulsion drive vibrates beneath me. "Comms are down since this storm rolled in." I think about the pre-recorded report I found. He pulls back on the yoke, and I sink into my seat.

"Blind approach it is. Let's hope that Mother's where she belongs once we clear the atmosphere." Willoughby pokes two fingers at the screen, increasing thrust.

We climb rapidly and break through the storm clouds. I watch the frozen methane split and slough off the lander's skin. I remember our fourteenth birthday when Mom took me up in a hot air balloon without Josh. He was too sick by then. In the distance, I see a glimmer at the edge of the atmosphere. It's Mother.

Anticipation.

"Right where she belongs." He opens the comms again. "Mother, this is Ares-1. Do you copy?"

No response.

"Run a diagnostic," he says.

I run it. Comms flash red. I rotate the display toward him. "Probably damaged by the storm." Or someone who prefers escape to death. I see Josh's face moments before his death. Pale and gaunt. So many tubes.

Sorrow.

"We can still dock without comms." He brings up a submenu on his screen and initializes auto-dock.

Opportunity.

"Thank you, Commander Willoughby. You've made this much easier." I unlatch my seat belt and rotate toward him.

"Made what easier? You need to stay buckled in. Stearns. Oh, God, no."

Ascension.

I wipe the last bit of blood from the pilot's seat and toss the rag atop what's left of his body in the airlock and vent the whole mess into space. As Ares-1 docks, I shut down the engines. I remember flight school, saying goodbye to family, and this deep-space mission. I delete the log of my opening the airlock, then wait for Mother to receive me.

My secret is secured.

I check my new face and its dark eyes in the mirror before the doors open.

The captain greets me. "Sixteen hours without contact. We nearly lost hope. What the hell happened down there, Willoughby?"

"There was a storm. We lost comms. I lost Trask to exposure and Stearns to terrain. She left a report."

"Are you injured?"

"I'm fine, just exhausted and hungry."

"And maybe in shock?" He looks down his nose at me. "While you were gone, we got word from Earth." He clapped me on the shoulder. "We're headed home."

I remember Willoughby's home. No, my home in Vancouver. I smile.

Freedom.

Speaking of Clouds

by Juli Simon

My world, at night, is a kingdom
of clouds.
Time and tides still pulse and pull,
but gently;
encouragement in nods.

The memory of clouds
is deep enough to climb.
The hills thick, indistinct,
and alive
to suggestion.

I walk inside the walls: mist-made and
soundless as snow.
I arrange them
with the pressure of one small hand.
Pillow drifts, mine to touch; impossible
to hold.

I remain steadily myself,
a familiar visitor,
and they soften
to welcome me, finally to sleep.

So safe till
morning comes,

cloudless
and bright.

There is breakfast
and toothpaste, and
clothes all laid out:
appropriate for
bus rides and school halls
and people who
never
once
speak of clouds.

Help Wanted #8

by K. L. Small

Brianna shoved her hands in her jeans pockets and trudged down the back alley toward her small studio apartment. She kicked a dilapidated cardboard box that blocked her path. With a squeal, a gray rat scurried down the alley.

"That's right. Run away!" The words tore at her heart. Returning to Iowa felt like running away from her dream of success on Broadway. But what else could she do? She was unemployed and behind in her rent.

She passed the back door of the tattoo parlor, then glanced at the grimy window of the narrow shop next door that faced the alley. Its nondescript entrance was easy to overlook. The smudged lettering on the window read, Mydori's Mending. Why hadn't she noticed this shop before?

Brianna smirked. Who mended clothes these days? Her jeans had shredded knees, and she would never dream of patching them. Looking closer at the dirty glass, she noticed a small sign behind the window: Help Wanted—Inquire If You Dare. More curious than concerned, she reached for the door handle. The door swung open with a groan. A tiny bell jingled, announcing her arrival.

"Come in," a female voice called from the back.

After entering the dimly lit shop, Brianna closed the door. The bell tinkled again, and the sounds from outside faded. Lavender and sandalwood scents mingled in the air. She closed her eyes and inhaled deeply. This would be a pleasant place to work and so close to where she lived.

"I'm here about the job." Brianna raised her voice for the person who had yet to come into the room. She glanced around the tiny shop. Spools of thread were mounted on a display stand. A row of glass jars with buttons sorted by color lined a shelf. Several garments lay on a waist-high countertop. No sign of ribbons, laces, or bolts of fabric. A single empty chair sat near the dingy window.

"Very good." The thump of a cane against the floor and shuffling footsteps grew louder. An older woman, barely five feet tall, emerged from the back room. She wore a plain blue skirt and a white top with an embroidered neckline. A gray tabby cat trailed behind her.

"Are you the owner?" Brianna asked.

"I'm Mydori. Can you sew on a button?"

Feeling confident, Brianna smiled. "My grandmother taught me to sew. I worked as a stitcher for the costumer on Broadway," she lowered head, "until the show closed."

Mydori clumped across the floor to the chair by the window.

"I can patch a tear and darn a sock," Brianna continued.

"Useless skills." As Mydori settled in the wooden chair, she shook her head. "No one wants darned socks. Buttons. They want buttons. That's all I do."

Brianna narrowed her eyes. What kind of mending shop only did buttons? "I can handle buttons and buttonholes."

Mydori waved an arm toward the button jars. "Show me."

Brianna approached the jars with buttons in assorted sizes and shapes. Her fingers brushed the glass of the first jar with red and burgundy buttons. Warmth crept up her arm. Then she slid her hand to the container of green buttons with metal shanks. The taste of green mint made her open her mouth in surprise. At the smell of cut grass, she backed away from the jar.

Quickly, she glanced at the old woman. Mydori's head was bowed, her eyes closed. The old woman's gnarled hands shook with an irregular tremor. The cat sprawled on Mydori's lap; feline eyes fixed on Brianna.

She needed this job. The alternative was going back home to the small-town life she had escaped. Taking a deep breath, she grabbed a jar with wooden buttons. She removed the glass lid and reached in for the toggle button that caught her attention. When her fingers closed around it, she gasped. She stood in a dense forest with trees surrounding her. Branches shifted in the light breeze. A shaft of sunlight fell across her face.

"That will do nicely," Mydori said.

The trees disappeared, and Brianna stood trembling with the toggle button in her hand. "What happened?"

Mydori fished a packet of needles and a spool of brown thread from a basket by her chair. With crooked fingers, she offered them to Brianna. "Sew that button to the jacket on the counter."

With a nod, Brianna took the needles and thread. She picked up the jacket and spotted where a button was missing. She stared in shock at the remaining buttons, all wooden toggle buttons. They matched the one she held. Exactly!

Despite her shock, Brianna threaded the needle and sewed the button in place. As she stitched, the tension in her shoulders eased. She imagined herself in the woods with leaves rustling and birds singing. Peacefulness settled over her, and she hummed until she tied the final knot.

"All done." Brianna handed the jacket to Mydori.

The old woman stroked the button and nodded. "You're hired."

"Don't you want to know my name or have me fill out a form?"

Mydori leaned forward and rose slowly. "I know what I need to know."

"Okay," Brianna said tentatively. "How much do I get paid? What are my hours?"

Shuffling to the counter, the old woman reached into a metal box and removed a yellowed envelope. She handed it to Brianna without speaking.

After opening the envelope, Brianna's eyes widened. She leafed through the bundle of cash. There was enough to pay her back rent and most of next month's expenses.

"I appreciate this," Brianna stammered, "but it's too much for sewing on one button."

"Brianna, you did much more than that."

Brianna nearly choked. "You know my name."

"Of course. I've been waiting for you."

"I don't understand." Brianna rubbed her sweaty palms against her jeans.

"You will . . . in time," Mydori snorted. "After I teach you the secret."

Brianna swallowed and ran her tongue over her lips. She glanced at the envelope in her hand. What had she gotten herself into? The sign had warned: If You Dare.

"A secret?"

Mydori smiled at her. "I need to pass along my knowledge. My days of Cinderella gowns are over." She wiped a tear from her eye. "That was a mighty fine garment. But my fingers can barely hold a needle now. You're my new apprentice. I'll teach you about buttons."

Brianna furrowed her brow. "Buttons?"

"And other things." Mydori's laughter sounded like a cackle. The old woman nodded. "People pay dearly for my buttons. They're infused with magic. The right button will change the life of whoever wears it. And you have the gift."

"What gift?" Brianna recalled the warmth from the red button jar, the unexpected taste of mint, the smell of grass, and the forest experience. Could that be the gift?

"Another secret. More tomorrow." Mydori hobbled into the back room.

"I'll be back. You can count on that." Empowered, Brianna tightened her hold on the envelope. She removed the help-wanted sign from the window and left the shop. No running back home to Iowa. She would be a success in New York City after all, once she learned the rest of Mydori's secrets.

The Yellow Pencil #6

by Lona Smith

Thomas Dee Akins: February 7, 1895 – October 3, 1966

I watched my father put his hand in his pocket, pull out the contents, and lay them on the table as he did when it was time for his gray-and-white striped overalls to go into the basket for washing. There was, of course, his small pearl-handled knife that he used to trim his finger nails and whittle small wooden figures for us, odd nuts or bolts, an occasional unusual stone, a wadded, red bandanna handkerchief, which also went in the basket, *and* his yellow pencil. The pencil was short, maybe two inches long. The nub of rubber eraser that was left in its metal collar was darkened and pebble-like. A tip of graphite peered from a rough cone of wood at the opposite end, but bright-yellow paint, although smudged with grime, held fast to the hexagon-shaped sides.

"Why do you carry this?" I asked, picking it up. "You always have it in your pocket, but you don't use it."

"Oh, it's too short to use now," he said. He studied me for a moment. "I think it's time I told you a secret." He took the stubby pencil from me. "This is the only thing I ever stole."

I widened my eyes in disbelief. Tom Akins, a hard-working man of few words, was known in our community as a man of integrity, a man who kept his word, and could be counted on when help was needed. We knew he loved us but was uncomfortable with ways of showing it. "You got punished for showing feelings when he was growing up," my mother explained. The closest he ever came to crying was to swallow hard and turn away from sadness or pain.

Even though my sister and I would beg him and our aunts to tell us, I knew only sketches of my father's early life of growing up in Indian Territory before it became the eastern half of the state of Oklahoma. While it fascinated us, they were reluctant to talk about their shameful and hurtful childhood.

———

The Choctaw tribe of Native Americans was the first of five tribes to be moved from the Southeastern states of this growing country by the US Government in the 1830s. The Trail of Tears took them to a place called Indian Territory and the more than billion-year-old Ouachita Mountains. The Ouachita's rich veins of bituminous coal brought land developers, railroad tycoons, pioneers, and Europeans who worked in those coal mines. In addition, the dense vegetation and hidden caves of those old mountains were sanctuary for gangs of outlaws, cattle rustlers, train and bank robbers. My grandfather was one of those. The only law in the territory to bring these criminals to justice was the US Marshals and the posses they hired.

We knew that our grandfather and his sixteen-year-old bride, half his age, came by wagon train from Mississippi to escape punishment for crimes he had committed. We knew that the family frequently moved under the cover of darkness and changed its name to hide from posses looking for him. We knew that our grandfather had spent time in prison. Our grandmother, for whom I was named, was left to care for eight children. Pretending to be poor, she wore a money belt under her petticoat, hiding $150,000 that she was keeping for her husband when he came home.

What we didn't know was what it was like living with a man who had no regard for the law and was also a mean drunk.

———

"One day, this boy that sat behind me in school came to class with a whole box of long, yellow pencils," my father said. "We had never seen *yellow* pencils. There was maybe a dozen of them, all neatly lined up. He bragged that they were better than any others because the graphite came from China, and that they were painted yellow because in China yellow was a sign of royalty.

"One day, when he wasn't at his desk," my dad said, "I took one of those brand-new pencils out of that box. I don't think he ever missed it. Of course, I never could use it at school, and when my brothers and sisters asked where I got it, I lied and told them he gave it to me.

"Before long we moved again, changed our name, and Mamma enrolled us in a new school. At first, I liked showing off the pencil, but every time I sharpened it, I got this kinda sick feeling in my stomach."

"But Daddy," I said, "stealing a pencil is not such a terrible secret."

"Oh honey," he replied, "that's not the secret. When I wrote with it, I got to thinking, *was this the way my daddy started?* A thief has to start somewhere, and I made up my mind, then and there, that I did *not* want to be like the man who was my father. That was the last school I attended. By then, I was fifteen years old and in the eighth grade. I quit school and went to work to help take care of my brothers and sisters, but I've always kept this to remind me."

He took my hand and placed the pencil in my palm. "You keep it for me," he said closing my fingers around it, "because the secret is that every day you get to decide who you want to be."

"Oh Daddy," I said, throwing my arms around the waist of those dirty, pinstriped overalls. "I want to be like you."

He gave my shoulder a gentle squeeze. "You go on now. I've got to get these in the wash." He swallowed and turned away.

Through Nana's Eyes

by Tom Swartz

T he sun beat on our windows. Kids played football in the street
on hot and sticky summer afternoons in Syracuse, New York.
It was a football city, and touch football games took place in every
neighborhood. Teams recruited the best players. But no one wanted
me. I sat in our upstairs apartment in front of a very old upright
piano. The ivory on middle C and D had flipped off the keys years
before I sat before them. It was 1992, and the piano had been in
Nana's home since the late 1930s. I looked across the room to see
my grandmother.

"I hate playing the scales time after time. They bore me," I pouted.

"You hate them now, but when you play songs, you'll love them,"
my grandmother said. "Your dad was a great musician. If you want
to be like your dad, you must practice."

Football didn't matter in my house. Nana made me sit at the
piano every day. She hummed the notes she wanted me to play, and
when I played a song, she hummed along with the tune.

"Nana, I want to play with the kids downstairs. They know foot-
ball. If I don't play with them, I won't be good enough." She never
got mad. She smiled and said, "You can play with them after you
practice. Your dad had to peddle papers after school, so he got up
at five every day and practiced an hour before school."

My mom and dad died in a car accident when I was two. The
only memories I had were stories my grandmother told me. I was
lucky. I only lost the toes on my left foot in the accident. After the
funeral, Nana adopted me.

One day, after an hour of practice, I complained, "I've had
enough, Nana."

Nana bent down and placed her hands on my shoulders. "When your father was in ninth grade, he played a piano solo for his whole school."

"If you let me practice football, I'll be fast enough. All my friends play." I paused, then said, "Besides, Nana, I'm not ready to play in front of an audience."

She nuzzled her forehead against mine. "If you keep up your practice, you will be."

I was smaller than Mark and John, two of my classmates who lived in the apartment downstairs. They already made the modified high school team. One day, on the walk home from school, I said, "Mark, I want to play football. I love to throw and catch a ball. If I only could run faster."

"Look, Tom, you're a lousy football player . . . no offense. You can't run."

"But I-I. . ." I stammered.

"I don't mean to hurt you buddy," he said. "You're already a good piano player, and someday you'll be a great one. Stick to what you're good at."

For the next year I practiced piano, while my friends played sports. They practiced power right sweeps. I practiced adagio, allegro, and diminuendo. My nana hummed near the piano every practice. Christmas of my freshman year, I opened a long, heavy, gift-wrapped box beneath the tree.

"You've earned your present, Tom."

"Wow, Nana, I can't believe it. It's a Yamaha!" The full keyboard had eighty-eight shiny keys.

"I'm ready to play in a band with this baby."

A few weeks later, on my thirteenth birthday, I asked two juniors in the music department, a guitarist-bass player and a sophomore drummer, to join me. As my high school years went by, my friends did all right on the football field, but I played solos for almost every school concert, played in the gym for our dances with my group, and became one of the most popular kids in my class.

By my senior year in high school, my band won a talent contest on the local television station and traveled to Bermuda. The station booked us to play in various venues in Hamilton, and the notoriety helped me win a scholarship to Syracuse University's School of Fine Arts.

After college, I played at well-known jazz platforms in America: Birdland and Blue Note in Manhattan; The Famous Open Door and The Palm Court in New Orleans, and the Pershing Jazz Club in Chicago. After three years on the road, I met Pearl, the woman I would marry who taught music at my college alma mater.

Life isn't all happiness. We meet disappointments and obstacles along the way. On my first year back, Nana—my only parent, piano teacher, and cheerleader—was stricken with cancer. Months of chemo and radiation, diets and exercise regimens, sapped her strength and ultimately failed her.

One day, Nana called on my cell phone and asked me to see her. The next afternoon, I came to her bedside. We had moved her near the front room window and closer to the bathroom.

"Tommie, I've loved you since I first held you in my arms, and now you've become such a fine man."

"I love you, Nana, and thank you for all you have taught me, especially the piano. Without my dad's gift, I would have struggled in life."

"You're a talented guy. You fought me for months before you realized you loved music."

"I know, Nana, but dad's musical ability pulled me through."

"Oh, Tommie, it's time I told you my secret." She struggled to sit up under the blankets around her. "You wanted to be like your dad who was a good athlete, but an awful piano player. You had no memory of him, except through my stories. I told you he was a great musician, so you had a target to aim for as you built your skills."

"You lied to me all these years?"

"You struggled and felt unworthy because of your foot injury. I knew you had greatness within you, if you looked in the right places."

I swallowed hard. "Nana, you had to trick me into my practices? What kind of person was I?"

"Tommie, I couldn't reach you . . ."

"I was young, but unworthy?" My eyes filled.

"You were young and wanted to be an athlete. I wanted you to choose a skill you could master. I didn't lie to you; I inspired you."

"Nana, I know it. You did inspire me." I reached for her hand and kissed it.

She slid over to the edge of the bed and took my other hand. "You forgive my deception?"

I held her and inhaled her cologne's sweet apricot smell. "Oh, Nana, I love you. I need to understand the secret you held all these years."

She lifted my hands and kissed them. She said, "My stories pushed you forward all these years." Tears filled her eyes. "They were for your good, not mine. I hope that makes a difference."

I smiled and held her. "Your secret was an act of love, and I'm grateful to you."

She curled into my arms, and I felt how slight and frail she'd become.

She closed her eyes, hummed one of the tunes we often practiced together, and fell asleep.

The next day Nana slipped away.

Whispers

by Skye Taylor

My humans think just because I'm a dog, I don't know they're talking about me and keeping secrets. Normally, I wouldn't be too worried, but I like to know everything that's going on. I don't like secrets.

When Milo and I were puppies, they spelled things out so we wouldn't know when a treat was being considered. But dogs are smarter than our humans think. It didn't take us long to learn that W-A-L-K meant we were going out. Or R-I-D-E meant a trip in the car. When we grew up, they quit trying to fool us. Now they just say "walk," and I hurry to get my leash, and if I hear the word "ride," I'm at the door before they've even got their coats on.

But something changed a few months back. They started talking about a trip to a place called the Rainbow Bridge. Milo and I were all excited. We like trips, even if it's just to the place where they get food. Vacations are even more fun. Once we went to Vermont and went over a thing our humans called a covered bridge. Kind of weird driving through a house and out the other side, but they seemed pretty impressed with it. The best part of that trip was the snow. Milo and I had never seen snow before, but it was almost as much fun as swimming at our beach. Anyway, that was the only bridge they ever talked about until a couple months ago.

Suddenly they were whispering about this Rainbow Bridge place. Even Milo had no idea what they were talking about in the hushed worried whispers, and he's the one who got to go with them when they found out about the place. I got left home that day. And a bunch of other days after that. Always with a pat on my head and the promise they'd be home soon, and off they'd go with Milo. When they came home, there was the scent of other dogs on their clothes, but Milo didn't seem concerned about that, so I didn't think much of it. I was more worried that they were keeping secrets.

Even more worrying, Milo wasn't feeling like his old self. I have no idea if it had anything to do with this place they took him where they all came home smelling of other dogs, but it was clear Milo wasn't well. I brought him his favorite toys, but he didn't want to play. He didn't want to go swimming with me either, and that was even odder than all the whispering. Milo loved the water more than I do. More and more often, he just curled up on the big, fluffy bed we shared and closed his eyes when I went outside to go swim alone. I cut my swims short, so I could hurry back to him. I'd shake as much of my wetness off as I could, then go curl up next to him and keep him company.

The last time I saw Milo, our humans patted me on the head like they always do. They said they were going to the Rainbow Bridge, and they'd be home soon. Only Milo wasn't with them when they came home. They hugged me more than usual, harder than usual, and there were tears running down their faces. I licked their tears and tried to make them feel better, but it was hard when I was missing Milo so much. Dogs don't make tears for sadness like humans do, but I felt sad inside. I didn't know where Milo went, and our big bed was so empty without him.

————

That was a few months ago, and lately we've all been more cheerful. Except, now the whispering has started again. No mention of that Rainbow place, but whispers just like when Milo went away and never came home. More secrets I might not like. Last week, they were gone for a really long time, and they were talking about me when they returned, pointing to my big lonely bed and at the basket of toys I used to share with Milo. And whispering.

There was more whispering this morning and a lot of extra hugs.

I really didn't like secrets. Maybe something bad was about to happen. Again. I curled up on the rug by the door to wait. I felt anxious. I wanted to close my eyes and sleep the time away, but I couldn't.

When the sound of car wheels crunched up the drive, I leaped to my feet, ears perked.

Laughing and happy sounds. I relaxed a little.

The key clicked in the lock, then—

"Hey, Max. Come on out, and see who's here."

Didn't have to ask me twice. I loved company.

But there were only two pairs of legs on our front walk. Puzzled, I pranced over to get a pat and some reassurance.

"We've brought you a surprise, Max," my human said as he squatted down. "Meet Murphy."

And a wriggling ball of fluff tumbled from his arms onto the walkway at my feet. A baby version of me. My heart raced as I gave this mini me a thorough sniffing. He licked my paw, then sat up and waved his paws toward my face. Was this what all the whispering had been about?

I did a downward doggie, so I could look the little fellow in the eye. He rolled over onto his back, so I gave him another thorough sniffing. Then in a flash, we were running and tumbling all over the front yard. I felt younger and happier than I'd felt in months.

Murphy's just a pup, so he was ready for a nap long before I was, but that's okay. I can show him around and introduce him to everything later. He'll get bigger, and just think of all the adventures we can share together. I can teach him to swim. I'll even share all my toys.

Our humans called us into the house where I showed Murphy my big, empty bed. He climbed right in, curled up, and closed his eyes. Now it's *our* bed. I went back to lick my humans' hands. I wanted to thank them properly for the wonderful new surprise. Then I went and curled up with Murphy.

This was a good surprise. And I'm going to love Murphy just like I used to love Milo.

The Fairy's Wheel

by Bobbie Thiessen

T he man at the gate smiled as a tall, heavyset man approached, holding a dark-haired girl's hand.

"Floyd Townsend, as I live and breathe," he said, clapping Floyd on his back. "And who is this little thing?"

"Johnny, this is my granddaughter, Mary Beth, Holly's daughter."

Johnny's smile grew larger as he noticed the two women who had walked up behind Floyd and Mary Beth. "My goodness, Holly May. It seems like just yesterday you were not much bigger than this little one. And, Miss Ruth," he nodded at the older woman, "it's so nice to see you, again."

As Floyd opened his wallet, Johnny shook his head. "Oh no, you don't. I'm not letting one of our former carnies pay for tickets. Here you go." He handed Floyd a long narrow stream of tickets. "Come back and see me if you need more."

"Thank you, Johnny," Floyd said. "Where's Sammy set up tonight?"

"Oh, he's in the back of the sideshow area running the hoochie coochie show."

The smells of popcorn, peanuts, and funnel cakes greeted the family as they entered the gate.

"What's a carnie, Grandpa?" Mary Beth asked.

"That's a person who works at a carnival."

"You work here?"

"Used to. A long time ago. I still stay in touch with some of the guys and come to see the carnival when it's in town."

"And, what's a hoochie—what that man said—show?"

"Hoochie coochie shows are just a bunch of women carnies dancing."

The smells grew stronger and the noises louder as they passed the food vendors and the game stalls. Mary Beth jumped when a man at the strongman game made the puck ring the large bell. Those around him cheered loudly. More cheering came from farther down the midway where a teenage boy with greasy, brown hair threw darts at balloons.

"Step right up, little missy, and pick a duck for a prize," one carnie called out as Mary Beth's family neared his stand.

"Can I, Grandpa?"

"Sure." Floyd handed two tickets to the worker.

"See the ducks floating by? Just pick up one, and hand it to me," the worker instructed.

Mary Beth did as instructed and was soon hugging a small orange-and-green stuffed dog.

The family continued toward the sounds of music, shouts, and laughter until they reached the children's rides. Mary Beth smiled as they neared the carousel featuring brightly painted horses. Her eyes widened more when she caught sight of the Ferris wheel.

"Ooh, what's that ride?"

"That's a Ferris wheel..."

"You're too little for that ride," Holly spoke up. "You'd get scared and try to jump out."

"No, I wouldn't," Mary Beth said.

Ruth led Mary Beth to the carousel, and soon the little girl was riding a pink-and-purple horse.

Mary Beth and her grandmother rode most of the children's rides that night, and sometimes Holly rode with them. Floyd talked with several of the ride operators as he watched his granddaughter experience her first carnival.

"I really wish I could ride the fairy's wheel," Mary Beth confided in Ruth as they disembarked from the train ride. I'm not afraid of being up high like Mama."

Ruth nodded. "I know, Mary Beth. I got your mother to ride when she was a bit older than you. When it stopped at the top, she got so scared, she tried to jump out."

"That's dumb," Mary Beth whispered to her grandmother. "Mama's afraid of everything. She doesn't want me to swim in the big pool because she's afraid of water. She wouldn't let me cook marshmallows like the other kids because she's afraid of fire. It's not fair."

"No, it isn't," Ruth agreed as the two returned to Holly's side.

"Mama, can I please ride the fairy's wheel? I promise I won't try to jump out." Mary Beth looked up at her mother. "Please?"

"You mean the Ferris wheel? No. I told you, you're too little."

Floyd glanced at his wife. The two had been married for so long they could hold entire conversations without speaking a word. Ruth nodded so slightly that the movement was missed by Holly and her daughter.

"Well, let's go see if I can find Sammy's tent," Floyd said.

"You two go along. I'll take Mary Beth for one more ride on the carousel, and then we'll catch up," Ruth said.

"Come on, Holly. I know Sammy will be so pleased to see you again."

Holly and her father walked away. Holly glanced back once and saw her mother leading Mary Beth toward the carousel. Mary Beth patiently stood next to her grandmother as the line grew shorter. When they neared the ride's entrance, Ruth whispered to Mary Beth, "Want to ride the Ferris wheel?"

"Oh yes, Grandma!"

"You can't ever tell your mother. It will be our secret."

"But what about Grandpa? Can we tell him?"

"Yes, but not a word around your mother, or she'll never let us bring you to the carnival again."

Soon, the two were seated in one of the Ferris wheel's carts.

As the cart started its backward climb, Ruth asked, "You're not going to get scared and try to jump out, are you?"

Mary Beth shook her head. The smells and most of the sounds faded as the cart climbed higher. Mary Beth squealed. "Grandma, it's so pretty. I can see everything." She turned her head from side to side, peering below.

"Grandma, I can see the horse I rode, and I see the real horses over there. Look." She pointed toward the corral where children rode Shetland ponies. "And I can see the gate where the nice man gave us papers for the rides. Oh, Grandma."

When the cart stopped at the very top, Ruth pointed toward the sideshow area. "That's where Grandpa and your mother went. Can you see them?"

"No. The people are so small. They look like bugs." The night breeze gently rocked the cart, but Mary Beth seemed not to notice. She sat in silence mesmerized by the lights and movements below her. As the Ferris wheel started again, Mary Beth turned to her grandma.

"Oh, Grandma. The fairy's wheel is so wonderful. We're high up like birds when they're flying."

As the family was leaving the carnival later that night, Holly turned to her daughter. "What was your favorite ride?"

Mary Beth glanced at her grandmother, then smiled as she exclaimed, "All of them!"

Paradise Falls #5

by Lynn E. Welsh

The whitewater always sounded so angry to me before. Now as I navigate my kayak through Heaven's Gate and the Blender—the Class IV rapids I never dared before—the river shouts, "Hallelujah, sister, amen."

Yesterday, even the Class II rills and ripples hissed curses, shared vicious secrets I couldn't quite overhear. Today, as I ease into the eddy behind White Arrow Rock and listen for voices echoing up the canyon, all I hear is the running water purring itself to sleep.

The river's depths once seemed as murky and black-hearted as the lava rock itself—cooled and hardened past any remembrance of its volcanic mother's heat, hard as my own father's heart, silent as lips that will never smile or speak again, lips that never learned how to smile at a daughter. Now, each emerald pool shines an invitation. But I can't linger. Soon someone will realize my kayak is missing. Soon someone smart will start searching downstream.

I roll under, just for practice, penetrating the water to hang upside down in its shocking chill, until the breath burns in my lungs, and the roaring in my ears drowns all sound. Rocking my hips just right, I brace my blade and snap my body back up onto the living river. Hope I can do it again when the time comes, when it matters.

A blackbird on an overhanging branch sings straight into my face; I pass so swiftly underneath it. Out of the shadows, into the light.

Then I hear a shout, "There goes a kayak. Is that her?"

Two men are on the cliff up ahead to my right, waving and pointing and scrambling down boulders, toward the spot where I planned to rest in the shallows behind Eagle Rock.

Maybe they're just hikers? But then I see the silver glint on the short guy's blue shirt. And his bullhorn doesn't look like it belongs to a friendly forest ranger.

"Hey, are you Georgia Taylor?" the short guy shouts. "Hey . . . your father . . . we need—" The river swallows the rest of his words.

My father. Crushed under the tumbled woodpile, half buried by a dozen un-split oak logs. His own favorite ax sunk deep into his leg. That wasn't planned. That was a bonus.

Focus. There's no way the sheriff or deputy can reach me or stop me. I'm in the middle of the river, safe from everything except what lies ahead.

The water makes haystacks over sunken boulders, but I know how to read the waves, survived all my old man's lessons, learned the hard way how to dodge and weave, make myself scarce. But he always found me, no matter where I hid. Until yesterday.

My father knew all my secrets, except the last one. Those guys on the riverbank, they don't have a clue.

Something hidden underwater snags my kayak. It's a branch with long fingers that tries to hold onto me, flip me over, but I push off with my paddle just in time to get centered again before the final rapid, a narrow cut of roaring white waves squeezed between two granite slabs: The Point of No Return. The name is so right on, I have to laugh in the few seconds before the river picks up even more speed, gathering its forces, giving me just enough time to choose my line.

On the right, lies a narrow rock-strewn beach—and two men, different ones I think, but there's no time to look. I have to swing hard to river left, where the current flows forced out of its natural path by the logjam straight ahead.

The river springs in one glorious leap of faith over its own fears, falling the height of five tall men, taking me with it.

My kayak plunges, bow down, into the pool below—deep into its clean, green heart. I let the water absorb the shock, then burst up buoyant, paddle raised high in both hands.

"Look at me, Daddy, look at me. Too bad you can't see how good I really am." That one moment is all I can allow myself. The real celebrating will have to wait until I disappear.

Time to turn the boat around and take my last beating. Spinning it takes all my strength, but I paddle hard, straight into the cascading water. Shocking cold pummels my shoulders and hammers on my helmet, and then I'm on the other side, behind the falls, floating in a secret oasis of calm.

Forcing my frozen fingers to pop my spray skirt, commanding my numb legs to work, I drag myself out onto the rough ledge behind the falls, pulling my kayak halfway up behind me. Next, I pry the lid off the hatch and retrieve the waterproof bag that holds dry clothes, food, flashlight, and $2,200 cash. It's all I have left, but it's enough to get me far.

Just for good measure, I slam my kayak onto the rocks, battering it in case the boulders downriver don't do enough damage. One last pat on the scarred red flank of the thing I love most, then it's time to shove the little boat toward the pounding water, where it dances under the cascade, then flips and passes through the curtain, to become a silent witness to what everyone knows: No one ever survives the ride over Paradise Falls.

I'll be safe across the border before they even imagine.

NextGen Writers

Baba

by Perla A. Anderson

Hello. My name is Randesh. I live in Mysuru, India, and I lead an extraordinary life. I'm not rich or famous. I have not accomplished any great feats, but I have had the privilege of living with a wise man whom I call Baba.

Baba is my grandfather, a shopkeeper, and a pillar in our community. He opens his shop every morning at six a.m. to the sleepy-eyed commuters of the city. He sells everything one could want to eat while rushing off to start their day, such as fresh *paratha* made by the local women, crispy round puri and, of course, an array of chutneys. He also makes the most aromatic and delicious chai tea. Creamy milk mixed with warming spices and sugar served in a clay pot. These are common foods here in India, but my Baba makes them in such a way that crowds form only moments after he opens the door.

Today is Saturday, my favorite day of the week because I get to help Baba in the shop. If I am so lucky, one day I will run this shop that has been so diligently and lovingly maintained by Baba over the decades. I rise at four a.m. to complete my morning ablutions before we begin our busy day. On the way, Baba and I stop by the home of the four women who make the paratha that we sell in our shop daily. They have been tirelessly flipping the hot flatbreads through the night, so after our visit, they may finally find some rest.

The streets of Mysuru are filled with stray cats, garbage, and early risers on motorbikes. It isn't beautiful, but there is a peacefulness in the early morning that is lost once the sun awakens the rest of the city. We arrive at the shop and arrange the paratha in the window. Baba warms the milk for the chai, while I stir the chutneys made by mother and grandmother the day before. Although the shop will get busy soon, Baba always maintains his serene nature. He serves his customers, offers kind words to those who could use them and, at the end of the day, he gives what is left to the street people who accept his offerings gratefully.

Baba means grandfather, but it also means wise man. The name was given to him by the people of our community because he seems to embody something: a secret to life that not many know. He didn't pursue the spiritual or monastic path that is common here in India. Instead, he chose a simple life of serving the people with warm bread and hot chai. But what he really serves is something more than that, and it is just that mysterious quality that I want to know more about. I live with this man, yet he is more mysterious to me than the gods and deities that I learned about in early childhood.

We serve the people until early afternoon when he closes the shop. Today, Baba turns to me as we lock the door and says, "Randesh, I would like you to take over the shop for me one day when I no longer have the will to do it myself."

All I can say is, "Yes, Baba," though my mind is racing with thoughts of, *How could I ever run it as well as Baba?* And, *Will I ever be able to make the chai just right or make the puri so light and airy?*

Almost as if he could read my mind, Baba says, "I know you have doubts, but they will lessen once you learn the secret."

"The secret?" I ask.

"Yes, the secret of not only business, but to life. It is to serve others without thought of self. Once you can really do that, life becomes very easy, and success is sure."

I still didn't know exactly what that meant, but I knew that as the days and months passed, I would be shown. Not through a training program or manual, but from a living example: my Baba.

It Will Never Go Away

by Elizabeth Creve-coeur

No more hiding behind a graceful leap
Only to conceal the hurt that you can't keep
More than just physical pain, it's an emotional barrage
Everyone thinks it's easy, but they have no clue

How much it takes to put on a show, to dance through the pain
And pretend that you're not hurting, over and over again
Nobody sees the bruises and the scars, hidden from sight
Deceptive smiles and pretended joy—everything seems all right

With every graceful step, they take
The hidden pain they try to shake
Their heart's ache like a river's flow
Tears fall like raindrops on a window

All the pain that a dancer hides, it's never ending
Nobody realizes the agony that they're constantly tending
Gritting their teeth and forcing a smile, the show must go on
With each step they take, each leap they make, the pain will
never go away

My Secret Winter Wonderland

by Sage Kaleta

Every day while birds sing their songs in the forenoon
I sneak out to the shed that slowly falls apart each June
I go to my winter wonderland where life is at its fullest

As snowflakes fall, it foretells a future forever unforgettable
Leaving my world behind for this land may be regrettable
In this land of happiness, I'm reminded to live life to the fullest

I can feel the sunshine smiling softly down on me
And realize how the crystalline creatures that I see
Live in perfect harmony, living life to the fullest

Soon I must take my leave, knowing that my family
Will soon waken while this dream world remains with me
If only my family knew about how I live life to the fullest

A Secret for You: A Villanelle

by Hudson Lowe

Shhh, this is a secret for you from me
You mustn't tell a soul
It's quite incredibly fun, you surely must agree

I have a magic toy, it's not found easily
It's an awesome PS console
Shhh, this is a secret for you from me

When I turn it on with a very special key
Instantly it swallows me, falling through a tunnel
It's quite incredibly fun, you surely must agree

Transferred to the gaming world, it digitized me!
It takes me to a game where I don't have much control
Shhh, this is a secret for you from me

When I get achievements, the game might set me free
Like clearing all the blocks or making a soccer goal!
It's quite incredibly fun, you surely must agree

Sleepy as a sloth, I am tired, guaranteed
Now you know about my magic console
Shhh, this is a secret for you from me
It's quite incredibly fun, you surely must agree

Danger in the Waves

by Alexis Ollick

Hidden in the waves
A deadly secret danger lurks
Swimmers turn to slaves
Just simple swimming will not work

Swept out to sea
You tire, then drown
Send out a plea
Do not sink down

Tens of thousands per year get caught
Poor, unsuspecting people pulled away
The pull is stronger than they thought
"Help me, lifeguard!" is what they all say

They rip you away from comforting shore
Caused by waves swirling under at a sandbar
You may be strong, but the current is more
Hope you can escape before you go too far

Go swim along the shore, to the side
Never try to go back, don't fight
Once you're out, your options are wide
Paddle to shore and see the light

Don't die, by the rules above you must abide
This deadly phenomenon is recurrent

Mistakenly called undertow or rip tide
This secret villain is called a rip current

Adult Bios

Rose Angelina Baptista, a Brazilian American writer, is based in Central Florida. Her poems have appeared in or will soon appear in *Wallace Stevens Journal, João Roque Literary Journal, LitBreak,* and *Gávea-Brown: A Bilingual Journal of Portuguese-American Letters and Studies.*

Monika Becker is a former college professor who has authored many research articles but since retirement, she has concentrated on fiction writing. She has been published in ten Florida Writers Association Collections, placed in writing competitions, and made the Royal Palm Literary Award finalist list numerous times. She resides with her husband in Venice, Florida.

Paula Benski lives in Central Florida and writes as often as possible, usually at the expense of a good night's sleep.

Nancy Lee Bethea is Creative Writing Director at LaVilla School of the Arts in Jacksonville and a professional writer. She lives in Callahan, Florida with her husband, her daughter, a cat, and lots and lots of journals.

P.K. Brent writes dark fantasy, gothic, and paranormal romance. She was raised in upstate New York along the Canadian border. Eventually, she moved to northeast Florida where she lives with rescue cats and dogs.

William Clapper is a Bradenton, Florida-based former journalist who writes about ordinary people in extraordinary circumstances. He is a member of the Manatee Writers Group. He favors short stories and flash pieces—his work has appeared in the *The Florida Writer* and multiple Collections.

Scott Corey is the author of *Whistling for Hippos*, an award-winning memoir of his life in West Africa. His interest in international events and love of travel inspired him to live in Africa, France, Switzerland, Germany, and Sicily. Presently, he divides his time between Saint Augustine, Florida, and Europe.

Lynda Courtright enjoys stories of people facing life's challenges with bravery and humor and has written about such heroes in newsletter features and stories fictional and non. She lives on the edge of the Florida wilderness with the love of her life, several grown children, and two giant dogs.

Jennifer Reed Cox wrote other people's stories as her main source of income from 1980–1996. Some of those stories appear in the two books she co-authored as Ruth Joslin. In the last twenty-five years, Jennifer has written poetry and semi-autobiographical short stories with the dream of creating a novel.

Melody Dean Dimick is an award-winning author, a former high school English teacher at Northern Adirondack Central School, and an adjunct communication lecturer at the State University of New York at Plattsburgh. She serves as the President Emerita of the Florida Writers Foundation. She now publishes under her Coastal Cloud Watcher Press imprint.

Lynda R. Edwards wrote her first novel, *Redemption Songs*, after a reoccurring nightmare needed to find a voice. During the pandemic, she poured the uncertainty she felt into her second novel, *Friendship Estate*. When she reads, she wants to laugh, cry, and get mad! When she writes, she wants to feel the same emotions.

Elena Fowler writes poetry, short stories, and children's books. She enjoys walking the beach where she finds inspiration collecting shark's teeth.

Lorrie Gault is a retired DC corporate law AA now residing in Sanford, Florida. She enjoys writing humor in several genres. When not composing stories, she can be found playing bridge or relaxing with her husband and their many furry "children."

Carolyn Greeley is the award-winning author of *Emerald Obsession* and *Treasure Bound* (The Treasure Quest Series). Equal parts city slicker and beach bum, she concocts adventure-mysteries, combining contemporary action and historic exploits in an engaging escape. She lives in Saint Augustine, Florida. For more writing, join her newsletter at carolyngreeley.com.

Mark G. Hammerschick writes poetry and fiction. He holds a BA in English from the University of Illinois at Urbana-Champaign. His writing appears or will appear in various journals, including: *Calliope, Blue Lake Review, Naugatuck River Review, Grey Sparrow Journal*, among others. He residents in a northern suburb of Chicago and Naples, Florida.

Ellen P. Holder lives in Lake Wales, Florida. She has been published in several Florida Writers Association Collections and *The Florida Writer* online magazine. She writes novels, short stories, and poetry. She leads the Winter Haven Writers critique group.

Chris Holmes writes horror/romance and urban fantasy stories. She has three published novels, one novella, and several short stories. A graphic designer and freelancer, she designs her own book covers and has created hundreds of covers for other authors. Chris lives in Central Florida.

John Hope is an award-winning short story, children's book, middle grade, young adult, and historical fiction writer. His work appears in paperback, hardback, audiobook, and multiple short story collections. Mr. Hope, a native Floridian, gives informational and inspirational presentations to schools nationwide and bakes a mean apple pie.

Bart Huitema finally considers himself a long-time resident of Florida after dwelling in the Sunshine State for twenty years. He lives in the Bradenton, Florida, area with his teenage son and daughter. He's also a gadget guy and computer enthusiast who enjoys camping, boating, biking, and flying his drone.

Donald Jay writes mystery, adventure, romance, and inspirational stories suitable for all audiences. He enjoys treating readers to eclectic and engaging characters, unusual puzzles, and cleverly hidden clues. Formerly a magician, Don is also a woodworker, painter, and toymaker. His wife, Linda, says, "It's like being married to Santa himself."

Beda Kantarjian's short stories placed third in 2022 Porter Fleming, second in Bethune Short Story Competition, and have appeared in three anthologies. This is her twelfth Collection story, including a top-ten entry in 2013. Her creative nonfictions have placed first and second in the Royal Palm Literary Awards. She is co-founder/coordinator of Seminole County Writers.

Henry James Kaye, born and raised in Pittsburgh, had successful careers in banking, entrepreneurship, technology, and now real estate. His passion, writing, produced multiple Collection stories, several published novels, and two Royal Palm Literary Award winners. He married Nancy over forty-five years ago; they have three children and one grandchild. He lives in Longwood, Florida.

Tami Kidd has published three novels, and her poetry has been featured in two anthologies. She is an active member of the Winter Haven Writers Group and led the Crestview Writers Group before moving to Central Florida. She hopes to retire soon, so she can devote more time writing.

Michele Verbitski Knudsen hails from New Jersey but loves Florida and now calls Bradenton, Florida, home. Her new romantic mystery series is in the works. Michele hopes both mystery lovers and romance aficionados will enjoy the read, as fortune tellers, sumptuous culinary delights, and crazy relatives draw you into a tangled web of . . . murder.

Linda Kraus has taught university courses in literature and cinema studies. She has published poetry in several literary journals and anthologies and has published her first collection of poems, *Popcorn Icons and Other Poems Celebrating Movies*. She is an orchid judge, a film festival judge, and an impassioned rock-hound.

Andrea W. LeDew is a writer based in Jacksonville, Florida. She runs a blog of her own writing, "For Random Learning Comes." Her experiences as a parent, disability advocate, and recovering lawyer color her critiques of community, politics, and everyday life.

Joan Levy's favorite part of writing is revision, revision, revision. Is she crazy? She says the revision process leads her on a journey of discovery about the story and its characters. Levy is co-founder of the Seminole County Writers. Her stories have appeared in Collection anthologies and have won several Royal Palm Literary Awards.

Kimberly Lewis, a former United Methodist minister, retired educator, and new writer, has a BA in Speech Communication from the University of Georgia and M.Div. from Emory University. Her poems are published in the *Rise Up Anthology* and *Matter II, Volume 2* by Oprelle Publications. She lives in Kings Ferry, Florida.

Lawrence Martin is a retired physician, past president of Writers League of The Villages, Florida, and past Royal Palm Literary Award winner for short stories and full-length fiction. His writing includes books for both adults and kids.

Meredith Martin lives in Dunnellon, Florida, with her dog Mandy and cat Cali. When not reading, she likes to photograph sunsets and clouds, and to take walks with Mandy.

Robert E. Marvin is a member of the Florida Writers Association of Manatee County, and heads the Renaissance Writers group. He has been published in *Writer Advice, Writer's Type*, Florida Writers Association anthologies, *The Florida Writer* magazine and was a finalist in The Apparitionist National Ghost Story Competition.

Frank T. Masi has published stories in Florida Writers Association's Collections, *The Florida Writer*, and *Not Your Mother's Book* and has published poetry in *Revelry,* Florida State Poets Association's anthologies, and *Looking Life in the Eye.* Frank was the editor of *The Typewriter Legend* and published many business articles. He's currently writing a crime novel.

Phyllis McKinley, a former Canadian, lives in south Central Florida. In addition to five books, her work has been published from the pages of obscure poetry journals to several popular Chicken Soup Books. This marks her tenth contribution to the Florida Writers Collection.

Mark McWaters is a thirty-year advertising veteran with an MFA in Creative Writing from UNC-G. He is a past recipient of number one and number two placements in the Collection, a multiple Royal Palm Literary Award short fiction winner, and a first place Royal Palm Literary Award winner for unpublished novels in both Thriller and YA categories.

George August Meier focuses his writing on short stories. His work has appeared in *Amarillo Bay, Forge, Cleaning Up Glitter, Sisyphus, Hawaii Pacific, Newfound, Evening Street,* and other literary journals. He has degrees from Colgate University and The Ohio State University. He writes from the beach in Wilbur-By-The-Sea, Florida.

Barbara Meyers's novels mix comedy, suspense, and spice to cross the line between contemporary romance and women's fiction, and often feature a displaced child. Her latest novel is the paranormal romance, *Animal.* Visit her at barbarameyers.com.

Joanna Michaels writes fiction and memoir. The author of the mystery novel *Nun in the Closet*, she has been published in *CafeLit, Bright Flash, Drunk Monkeys,* and *Fine Lines*. She earned her MFA at Queens University of Charlotte and is a member of the Florida Writers Association.

Joan Wright Mularz writes young adult mysteries and also writes and illustrates picture books. She is a resident of Florida and spends summers in Maine.

Christopher Myers began storytelling professionally as a set designer for the Walt Disney Company, creating immersive visual environments for theme park attractions. He continues to develop the power of the visual by incorporating emotional elements as a scriptwriter. Presently, Christopher writes screenplays, nonfiction, and children's books.

Mark H. Newhouse, a former Florida Writers Association director, is a multi-year Royal Palm Literary Award medalist. *The Devil's Bookkeepers*, a suspenseful novel of love and courage during the Holocaust, was named Royal Palm Literary Award's Published Book of the Year; Gold Medal Historical Fiction winner, and Grand Prize Fiction Series winner in the Chanticleer International Book Awards.

Virginia Nygard, former Florida Writers Association group leader and regional director, has also held offices in the Vero Beach Branch of the National League of American Pen Women and is a member of the Florida State Poets Association. A published author, she has won numerous awards in several genres.

Mary Ellen Orvis is a retired attorney who lives in Sun City Center, Florida, where she enjoys writing, reading, and swimming.

Janet K. Palmer was born and raised in western New York State. She's also lived in Massachusetts and Michigan, before retiring to The Villages, Florida, with her husband, Mark. She enjoys writing, editing, reading, bowling, nature, her family, entertaining, decorating, Bible studies, and walking her two dogs.

Pamela Peffer lives on Florida's First Coast with her husband of many years. She is a devotee of historical fiction novels sprinkled with generous amounts of romance. As a beta reader, she recently discovered the delights of paranormal and horror musings. Her work has been published by Paramour Ink.

Paula Pivko started writing poetry at thirteen. She's been published in *The Florida Writer*, *Vulture and Doves, Social Issues for our Times*, and *Teen Angst*. Paula also was a finalist in the 2020 Royal Palm Literary Awards for poetry from the Florida Writers Association. She lives in Port Saint Lucie, Florida.

William R. Platt is a former advertising exec who loves speculative fiction. His short stories have been published in various anthologies and magazines including *The Florida Writer* magazine. He was included in the top ten of Florida Writers Association's *Collection 14, Thrills and Chills*. He currently serves as president of the Suncoast Writers Guild.

Stefanie Posteraro started her writing career documenting the Florida vibe as a journalist for community papers. She continues her work via articles, poetry, short stories, and photography. Stefanie graduated from the University of Florida College of Journalism and lives in Hollywood, Florida.

Barbara Rein writes "horror-lite" short stories (goosebumps, not gore) reflecting a childhood addiction to macabre fairytales and endless episodes of *The Twilight Zone*. Her book, *Tales from the Eerie Canal: 22 Stories of the Delightfully Dark and Creepy,* won the 2021 Royal Palm Literary Award for Published Book of the Year.

Allan K. Roit was born in Brooklyn. He received an undergraduate degree in History from Hunter College and master's degree in Political Science from Columbia University. For thirty-five years, he worked as a project manager for the US government. He retired to Florida with his wife and cats.

E.A. Russo is an author and professional editor who writes about culture, home, and reality with a healthy dose of optimism. She placed within the Florida Writers Association top-ten short stories of 2019 and was a Royal Palm Literary Award finalist for creative nonfiction in 2021.

Ruth Senftleber enjoys writing about interesting characters and everyday life. She is a Jacksonville, Florida, native, and her heart will always belong to Florida.

H.G. Silvia's passion for spinning mind-bending yet satisfying yarns that serve to entertain and be evocative are the goals he strives to meet in all his works. He is an active member of the Brandon Writers Critique Group. His primary focus is the completion of an upcoming novel.

Juli Simon is a professional muralist and amateur wife and mother living in Winter Garden, Florida, who has always found reasons to "write it down." In recent years, she has been prioritizing writing and finishing poetry.

K. L. Small writes fantasy stories for kids and the young at heart. Her books include: *A Dress to Remember: A Fairy Tale* and *The Magic Carousel* (Book 1 of The Brass Ring Series). She lives with her husband in Brooksville, Florida, on a horse ranch called Carousel Acres.

Lona Smith has been a member of Florida Writers Association for seventeen years. She is the published author of two novels, one biography, and numerous short stories. She is a recipient of two Royal Palm Literary Awards. She spends her winters on Amelia Island, Florida, and her summers in upstate New York.

Tom Swartz has written seven published novels and has been accepted in the Florida Writers Association Collection several times. He's a former Florida Writers Association board member, former Florida Writers Foundation president, and a proud member of the Seminole County Writers Group.

Skye Taylor is a former Peace Corps volunteer, a mom, a grandmother, and a great grandmother. She loves travel and adventure. She's jumped out of airplanes and been swimming with whales. She lives in Saint Augustine, Florida, where she enjoys writing stories that take flight and is an award-winning author of ten novels.

Bobbie Thiessen, a graduate of Virginia Commonwealth University, is originally from Virginia but has lived in Winter Park, Florida, for almost thirty years. She worked as a news and feature reporter for several Virginia newspapers before becoming a technical writer and instructional systems designer.

Lynn E. Welsh's story "Everything I Ever Wanted" won third place in the 2015 Royal Palm Literary Awards. Her story "365 Beds" was number ten in the 2015 Florida Writers Association Collection. Now retired from a career as a copywriter and creative director, she's refocusing on her writing and novel in progress.

NextGen Bios

Perla A. Anderson likes to surf with her dad and create fashion designs in her spare time.

Elizabeth Creve-coeur enjoys playing tennis and dancing ballet. She hopes to one day become a professional ballet dancer.

Sage Kaleta is a person that has dreamt of being amazing at archery and basketball.

Hudson Lowe is the oldest of three children. He loves jumping on his pogo-stick, playing outdoors (preferably when it's cool out), art, reading, algebra, and school.

Alexis Ollick is an eleven-year-old who describes herself as, "a boring, dumb, normal girl who hates cats and airplanes. SIKE!" She does high school classes and middle school classes at the same time; she aims to be a pilot, and absolutely LOVES cats!

Acknowledgements

As trite as it may sound, it really does take a village. In the case of the book you're holding, it's our village of Florida Writers Association volunteers who worked tirelessly to make this revamped version of our yearly anthology possible. At the foundation of this endeavor is our Data Management Chair, Elaine Senecal, who created the forms our entrants used to submit their fine stories and poems. Behind her is our VP of Administration & Membership, Michael Farrell, who coordinated the entries so that they ended up in my hands in a timely fashion. And thanks to Anne Dalton, Esq. who worked with me to draw up the writer's agreement that our authors were required to sign before publication in the Collection.

After I validated the entries, they moved on to our judge liaison, Arleen Mariotti, who sent the entries to our team of outstanding judges—who will all remain anonymous here, but to whom I give my highest praise. This year was particularly challenging, not only because of the number of entries each judge had to read and score—over thirty—but also because of the high caliber of writing they had to choose from. At least for me, it was heartbreaking to see some excellent stories not make it into Collection 15.

A very special thanks goes to our scorekeeper, Lori Palmer, who updated the scores on a daily basis and tallied the finalists.

Thank you to my fellow Manatee County writer Wil Clapper for his proofreading services.

Finally, as you hold this book in your hands, take a moment to appreciate the creative cover designed by Ginnye Cubel who also serves as FWA's Executive VP and Marketing Coordinator. And, as you read the stories and poems, know that the words would never have made it on the pages without the publishing expertise of Arielle Haughee, owner of Orange Blossom Publishing.

Florida Writers Association is truly a village of *writers helping writers*.

—Paul Iasevoli, Editor in Chief